THE GUITAR STYLE RESOURCE

a comprehensive guide to exploring new techniques and styles from heavy metal to jazz

RALEIGH GREEN

CD recorded by Collin Tilton at Bar None Studio, Northford, CT
Raleigh Green (guitar), Jesse Williams (electric and upright bass), Pete Sweeney (drums)

Cover photographs courtesy of (clockwise from top): Martin Guitar Company, Fender Musical Instruments, R. E. Bruné, Gibson Musical Instruments, Gibson Musical Instruments, and Schecter Guitar Research

Alfred Music Publishing Co., Inc.
P.O. Box 10003
Van Nuys, CA 91410-0003
alfred.com

ISBN-10: 0-7390-8908-0 (Book & CD)
ISBN-13: 978-0-7390-8908-8 (Book & CD)

Alfred Cares. Contents printed on 100% recycled paper.

CONTENTS

ABOUT THE AUTHOR 3

INTRODUCTION 4
  Basic Notation and Theory 4

CHAPTER ONE: The Guitar Styles Toolbox 6
  Lesson 1: Simplifying the Fretboard 6
  Lesson 2: The Octave Pattern 7
  Lesson 3: The CAGED System 8
  Lesson 4: Simplifying the CAGED System 9
  Lesson 5: Movable Fretboard Shapes 10
  Lesson 6: Using Scale Degrees to Build Chords 11

CHAPTER TWO: Rock Guitar 12
  Lesson 1: Palm Muting 12
  Lesson 2: Rock Chords 13
    Muting and Barring on the Fretboard 14
  Lesson 3: Rock Chord Shapes 15
  Lesson 4: Rock Chord Progressions 16
    Voice-Leading Labyrinth 16
    Three-String Strum 16
    Sweet Molasses 17
  Lesson 5: Rock Chord Embellishments 18
    Frost 19
  Lesson 6: Soloing in a Rock Style 21

CHAPTER THREE: Blues Guitar 23
  Lesson 1: Roman Numerals 23
  Lesson 2: The 12-Bar Blues 24
    Basic 12-Bar Blues 24
    The Chile's Gone 25
  Lesson 3: The Blues Shuffle 26
    The Troubled 8-Bar Shuffle 26
    Stevie's Shuffle 28
  Lesson 4: The $\frac{12}{8}$ Blues 29
    Cloudy Day Blues 30
  Lesson 5: Soloing in a Blues Style 31

CHAPTER FOUR: Acoustic Guitar 33
  Lesson 1: Slash Chords and the Bass/Strum 33
    Afternoon Again 33
    Absolutely 34
  Lesson 2: The Quintessential Strum 35
    Half a Strum to Play 35
    A Twist of Lime 35
  Lesson 3: The Muted Strum 36
    Fret-Hand Mute 36
    Take a Seat 36
    Moments Like Those 37
    Flap 37
  Lesson 4: Tricky Strumming Simplified 38
  Lesson 5: Acoustic Soloing 40

CHAPTER FIVE: Fingerstyle Guitar 42
  Lesson 1: Pick Your Variation 42
  Lesson 2: Fingerpicking Potential 45
    Passenger Pigeon 46
  Lesson 3: Travis Picking 47
    Travis Rag 48
  Lesson 4: Melodic Fingerpicking 49
    Fingerpicking Paradise 49

CHAPTER SIX: Classical Guitar 50
  Lesson 1: Posture and Positioning 50
  Lesson 2: Classical Fingerpicking 52
  Lesson 3: The Renaissance and Baroque Periods 53
    Greensleeves 53
    Cello Suite No. 1 (Prelude) 53
    Minuet in G 54

  Lesson 4: The Classical Period 55
    Etude in A Minor 55
    Allegro in G 55
    Prelude in C 56
  Lesson 5: Flamenco Guitar 57
    Rapid Rasgueados 57
    Flamenco Fingers Flying 57

CHAPTER SEVEN: Metal and Shred Guitar 58
  Lesson 1: Metal Rhythm 58
  Lesson 2: Tremolo Picking 60
  Lesson 3: Drop D and Odd-Time Riffs 62
  Lesson 4: Neo-Classical Metal 63
    Malmsteen Madness 65
  Lesson 5: Shredding Tricks 66

CHAPTER EIGHT: Reggae and Ska Guitar 68
  Lesson 1: Reggae Chord Voicings 68
  Lesson 2: Reggae Rhythm Chops 69
  Lesson 3: Single-Note Syncopations 70
    Rastafari Police 71
  Lesson 4: Third Wave Ska 72
    Don't Come Toasting 72
    More Than Inspired 72
    Dr. Bosstone 72
    Sub-Lime 73
    Reel Big Sale 73

CHAPTER NINE: Funk Guitar 74
  Lesson 1: Single-Note Funk Lines 74
    Funky Strut 75
  Lesson 2: The Chicken Scratch 76
    Feeling Funky 76
  Lesson 3: Building Chord Extensions 77
  Lesson 4: Funky Rhythm Guitar 78
    Theme Park Funk 78
    Bag of Potatoes 79
    Funk Machine 80
    Super Funky 80

CHAPTER TEN: Jazz Guitar 81
  Lesson 1: Jazz Chord Progressions 81
    How New the Key 82
    Chords in the Afternoon 82
    Some Keys You Play 83
  Lesson 2: Soloing Over ii–V–I Progressions 84
  Lesson 3: Jazz Blues & Walking Bass 85
    Bop Blues Stroll 85
  Lesson 4: Soloing Over a Jazz Blues 86
    Bebop Blues Solo 86
  Lesson 5: Jazz Chord Inversions 87
    Fall Inversions 88
  Lesson 6: Adding Color to Your Chords 89
  Lesson 7: Latin Jazz 90
    How Syncopated 90
  Lesson 8: Modal Jazz 91
    Modal Impression 91
  Lesson 9: Modal Jazz Soloing 93
    Tonal Modal 93
  Lesson 10: Jazz Soloing Strategies 94
    Maybe 94
    Outward Inclination 94
    Yellow Noon 95
    Not Just Acquaintances 95

Conclusion 95

Guitar Fretboard Chart 96

ABOUT THE AUTHOR

Raleigh Green is proficient in many styles of music and is an expert in MIDI guitar and music technology. He teaches guitar at Phillips Academy in Andover, Massachusetts and is a long-time instructor at the National Guitar Workshop in New Milford, Connecticut as well as DayJams in Boston. He performs regularly with Boston-based bands and teaches online guitar lessons at WorkshopLive.com.

Raleigh received a B.F.A. from the University of Missouri in computer-aided art/multimedia and graduated *summa cum laude* from Berklee College of Music, where he was honored with the Quincy Jones Award and the Professional Music Achievement Award. Raleigh has studied with world-class guitarists, including Jon Damian, Bret Willmott, Mick Goodrick, and jazz piano maestro Charlie Banacos.

Raleigh and his wife Laura live in Medford, Massachusetts with their Australian cattle dog Max.

PHOTO BY BILL SAMPLE COURTESY OF WORKSHOPLIVE.COM

Acknowledgements

Very special thanks to David, Barbara, and Jesse Smolover for their support of the arts; Nat Gunod, Burgess Speed, and everyone else in the Workshop family; the Breretons; and all of my students and colleagues who provide unending friendship and inspiration. Also, many thanks to my parents Ken and Linda Green for a lifetime of support and encouragement, and to Laura, my wife and musical partner.

Track 1

A compact disc is included with this book. This disc can make learning with the book easier and more enjoyable. The symbol shown at the left appears next to every example that is on the CD. Use the CD to help ensure that you're capturing the feel of the examples, interpreting the rhythms correctly, and so on. The track number below the symbol corresponds directly to the example you want to hear. Track 1 is a tuning track that will help you tune your guitar to the CD.

INTRODUCTION

This book is written for guitarists of all levels who are interested in broadening their horizons by learning to play in a variety of musical styles. *The Guitar Style Resource* is an instructional survey of many musical genres, with specific riffs, tricks, chords, scales, techniques, and examples unique to each style—a perfect companion for the weekend strummer or gigging professional. Whether you play a steel string, nylon string, electric, acoustic, solid body, hollow body, archtop, or flat top, this innovative method will lead you through historical, present-day, and emerging guitar styles, including rock, jazz, Latin, fingerstyle, classical, blues, reggae, metal, and more.

The first chapter of the book presents a unique method of visualizing shapes on the guitar fretboard. Mastering the fretboard is essential to becoming a versatile guitarist. The ability to quickly and accurately locate notes, scales, and chords on the fretboard is always important, no matter what style of music you play.

The following nine chapters represent nine different musical genres. Each of these chapters is filled with stylistic examples that progress from easy to medium to advanced. These chapters do not need to be studied in the order they are presented. Depending on your personal inclinations, feel free to skip around from style to style, using the introductory chapter as a reference.

While enjoying great sounding music and adding to your repertoire, you will increase your technical skills, your understanding of theory, and your musical capacity. However, to get the most out of the book it would be beneficial for you to have some experience with basic open chords and common major and minor barre chords. In addition, while knowing how to read standard music notation is not absolutely necessary, it would be helpful to have some familiarity with tablature (TAB) and basic music theory. Starting at the bottom of this page is a guide to some of the notation and theory used in this book.

As a practicing guitarist, you are ultimately in charge of your own musical path. Becoming an informed musician, trusting your intuition and enjoying the learning process are the keys to fulfilling your creative destiny. Get ready, because musical versatility is not just for studio musicians and composers. It's for anyone who wants to be a well-versed guitarist, able to play over anything. For the open-minded guitarist, the possibilities are truly limitless!

Basic Notation and Theory

Reading Tablature

Tablature, or *TAB*, helps you find notes on the fretboard. Tablature is written on six horizontal lines. Each line represents a string on the guitar, with the top line representing the 1st string (high E) and the bottom line representing the 6th string (low E). The numbers written on the lines represent the fret where each note should be played. The numbers below the TAB staff represent the left-hand fingering. (The fingers of the left hand are numbered 1 through 4 starting with the index finger.)

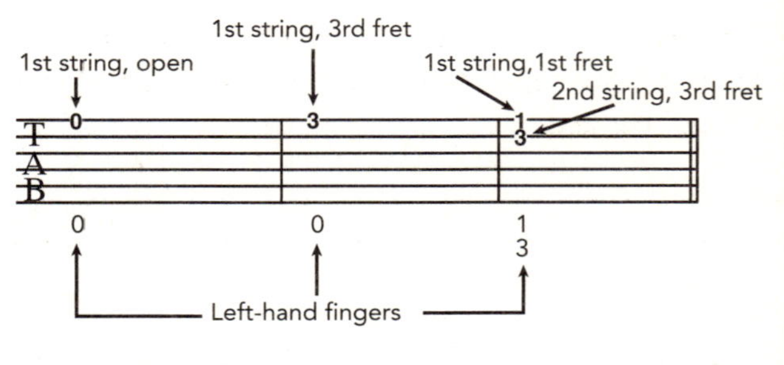

Rhythmic Notation

Rhythmic notation indicates rhythm but not pitch. This is often used to communicate strumming patterns for chords.

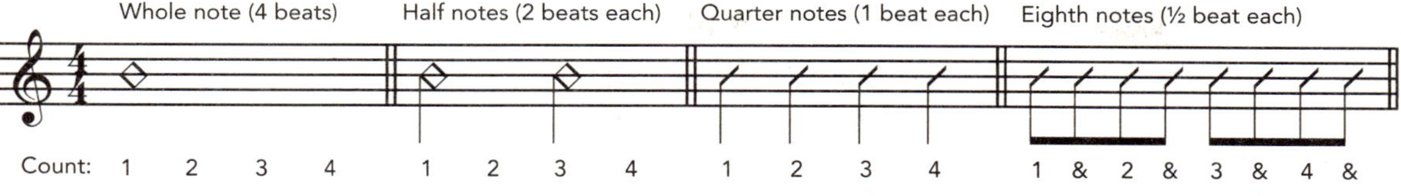

Reading Scale Diagrams

The top line of a scale diagram represents the 1st (highest) string of the guitar, and the bottom line the 6th (lowest) string. The vertical lines represent frets which are numbered.

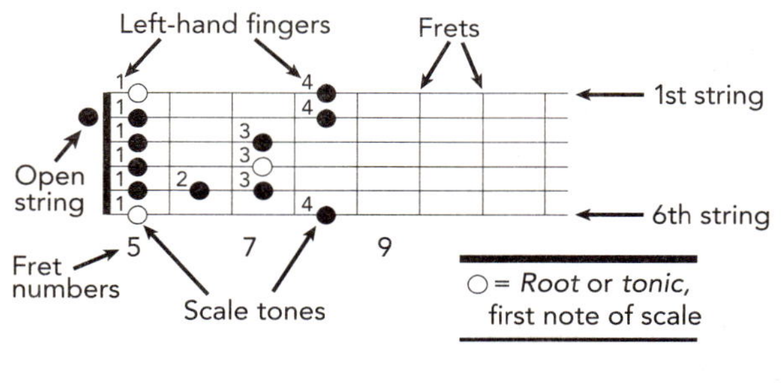

Reading Chord Diagrams

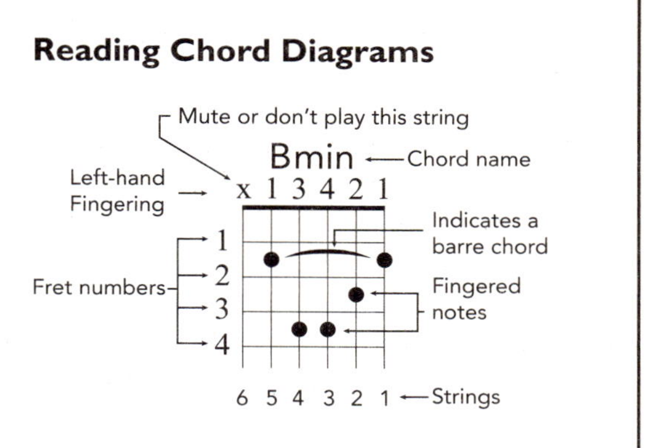

Fine: End the piece here the final time through the form.

D.C. al Fine: Go back to the beginning of the piece and play until you get to the **Fine**.

◼ = Downstroke
V = Upstroke

Major Scale Theory

A *scale* is a series of notes in a specific order of *whole steps* (two frets) and *half steps* (one fret). Each note of a scale is a *scale degree* and is given a number (1–2–3–4, etc.). The major scale is important because it helps us understand many musical concepts. It has seven notes in the following order of whole steps (W) and half steps (H): W–W–H–W–W–W–H. For example, below is a C Major scale. Note that the eighth degree (8) is the *octave* of the *tonic* (first note of the scale). An octave is the distance between two pitches of the same name.

C Major Scale

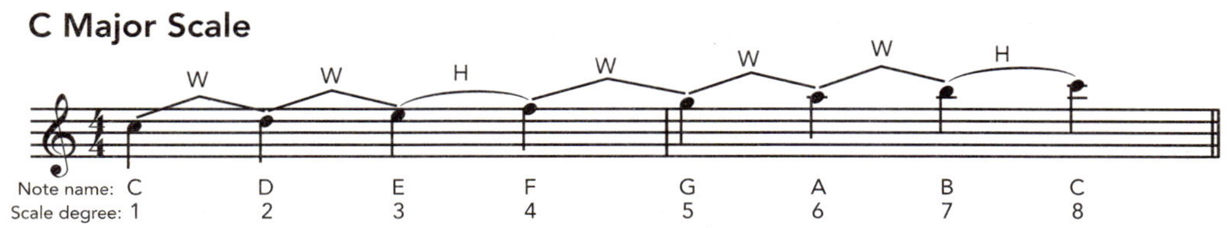

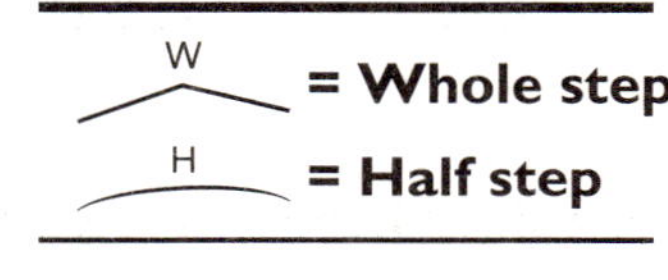

There are 12 different major scales. Each one starts on a different note of the *chromatic scale,* which is a 12-note scale with each note separated from the next by a half step. There is only one chromatic scale, and it contains every possible note on the guitar.

Keys

Keys get their names from scales. A key is made up of all the notes of the scale from which it gets its name. For example, the notes of the C Major scale make up the key of C Major. Because there are 12 different major scales, there are also 12 keys. (Technically, there are 15, if you count the *enharmonic* keys. The term "enharmonic," or "enharmonic equivalents," refers to notes, scales, or keys that have the same pitch but are spelled differently; for example F♯ and G♭.)

CHAPTER ONE
THE GUITAR STYLES TOOLBOX

+ +

Through visual diagrams, this chapter clearly illustrates ways to simplify and organize fretboard patterns. The material discussed in this chapter is an important component to becoming a versatile guitarist because it addresses useful concepts dealing with fretboard mechanics that are applicable to all styles of music. Take a moment to look over the information in this chapter, keeping in mind that if you want to get to the music examples immediately, you are free to move on to page 12 at any time.

Lesson 1: Simplifying the Fretboard

It's important to form an understanding of how the guitar fretboard is organized. Learning the notes on the guitar can sometimes be a daunting task; however, with the following four tricks, note location is greatly simplified.

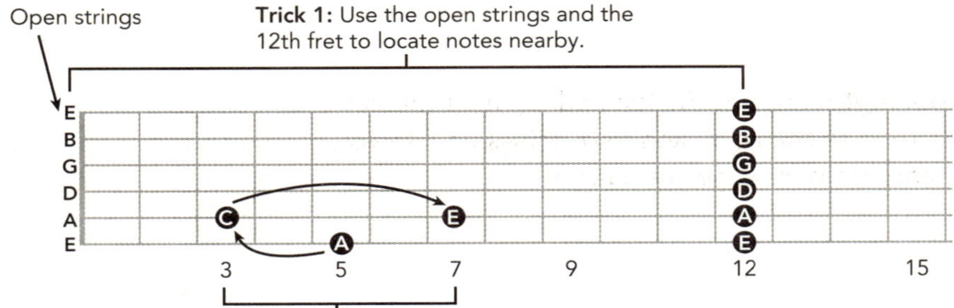

Trick 2: Use the notes on the 3rd, 5th, and 7th frets of the 5th and 6th strings to locate notes nearby. These notes are easy to remember because they make use of the fretboard dots on most guitars. Plus, when you connect them clockwise, they spell "ACE."

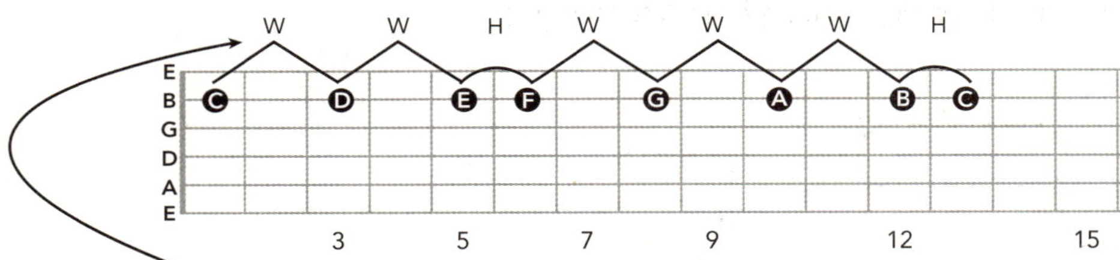

Trick 3: Build the C Major scale (see page 5) as a movable, one-string pattern of whole steps and half steps. You can think of the C Major scale as the white notes on a piano, which have no sharps or flats. Since there are no black or white keys to distinguish the notes on the guitar fretboard, the pattern of the scale (illustrated above) becomes very important. Internalizing this pattern will allow you to accurately visualize the C Major scale everywhere on the fretboard, because the pattern is the same on all six strings (starting from the note C).

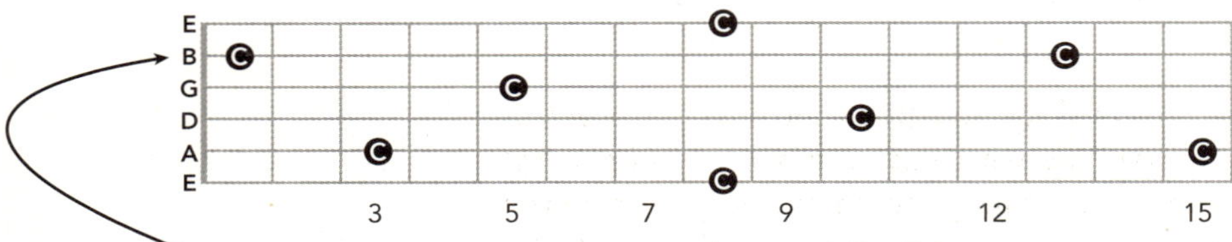

Trick 4: Use the octave pattern to get into familiar territory (the open strings, the 12th fret, or the "ACE") very quickly. Turn the page to explore the octave pattern in detail. Get ready, because this pattern holds the secret to fretboard freedom!

Lesson 2: The Octave Pattern

This diagram represents all the C's within a 15-fret span:

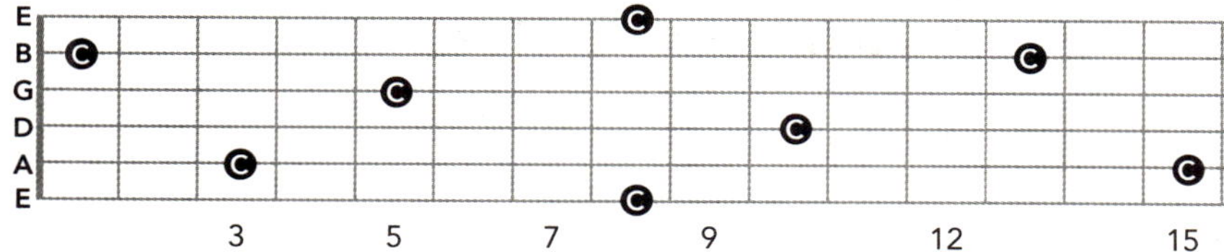

At first glance, the pattern above might seem like a fairly random collection of notes. However, if you visualize it from the right perspective, it is possible to simplify this pattern to only two simple shapes—a short rectangle and a long rectangle—that connect across the fretboard.

1) **Here's how to build the short rectangle:** Start at the left and connect the first note to the second by skipping two frets to the right, and two strings over. Do you see how the two notes create two corners of a rectangle?

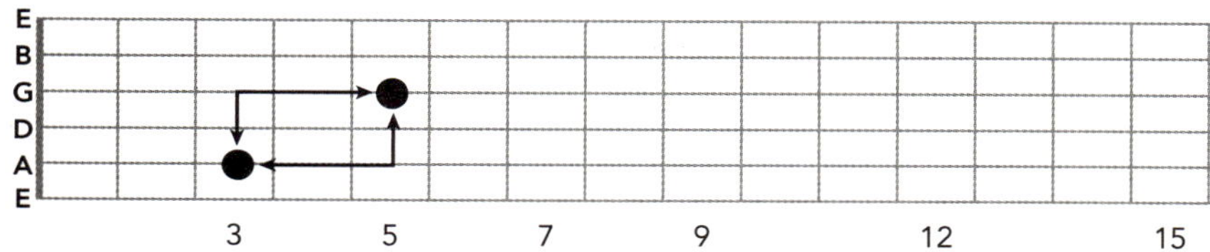

2) **Here's how to build the long rectangle:** Start at the left and connect the first note to the second by skipping three frets to the right, and two strings up. Do you see how the two notes create two corners of a longer rectangle?

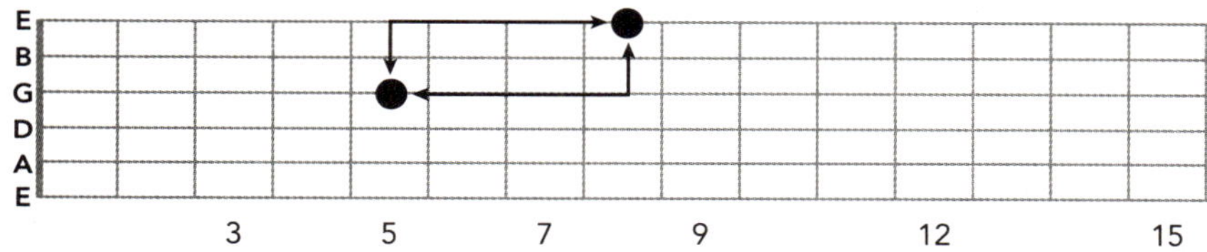

3) **Now, connect the two shapes together:** You can visualize this as one big shape outlined by the notes on the 5th, 3rd, and 1st strings (going from left to right).

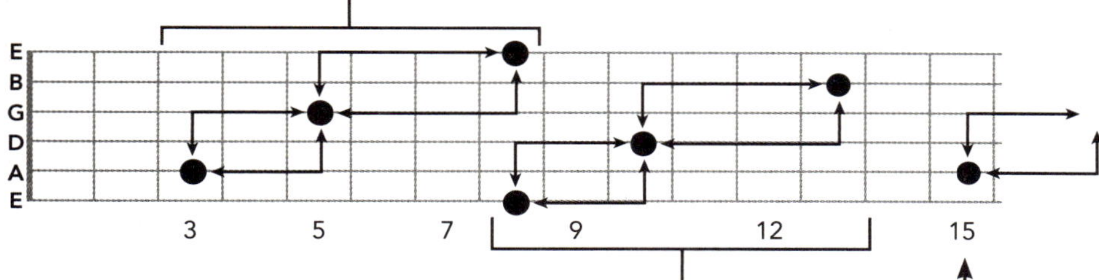

4) **Now, copy the whole shape to the 6th, 4th, and 2nd strings:** Notice how the last note of the first shape (on the 1st string) lines up on the same fret as the first note of the second shape (on the 6th string)? The shapes will always line up this way. You have now covered all six strings!

5) **Start the pattern over from the beginning:** Just go two frets to the right of the last note in the second shape, and start the whole pattern over. (This pattern repeats over the entire fretboard.) Here's the really good news: every note on the guitar follows this same pattern. For this reason, it's crucial to be able to shift the whole system up and down the fretboard, backwards and forwards. So, the next time you are faced with an unfamiliar note, ask yourself "what string am I on?" Then, refer to the pattern above to quickly move into familiar territory. Using this method, the open strings, the 12th fret, or the ACE shape will always be close by.

Lesson 3: The CAGED System

Have you ever wondered what would happen if you took a common C Major *triad* (a three-note chord composed of the root, 3rd, and 5th; in this case C–E–G) and plotted all three notes across the entire fretboard? Well if you did, you would get the *CAGED system*. This system provides a way to connect major chords across the entire fretboard by visualizing familiar open chords.

1) Build a C Major chord: 2) Use the octave pattern to locate all of the C's.

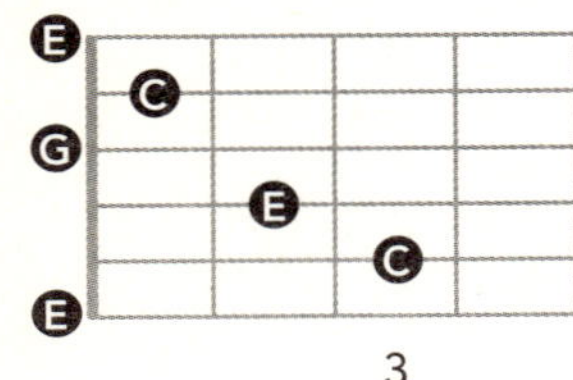

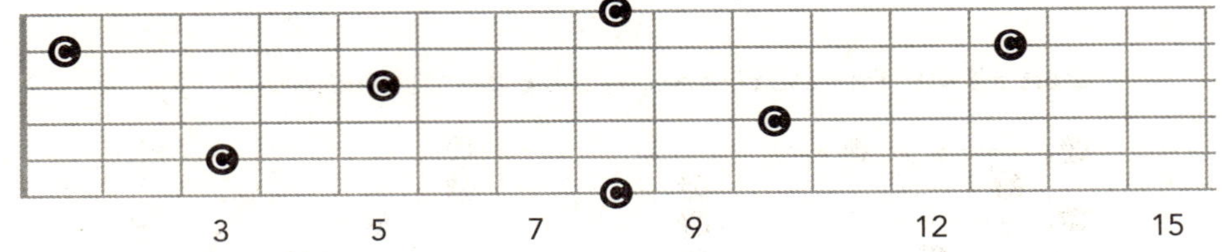

3) Use the octave pattern to plot out all of the E's and G's as well, and you get this collection of notes:

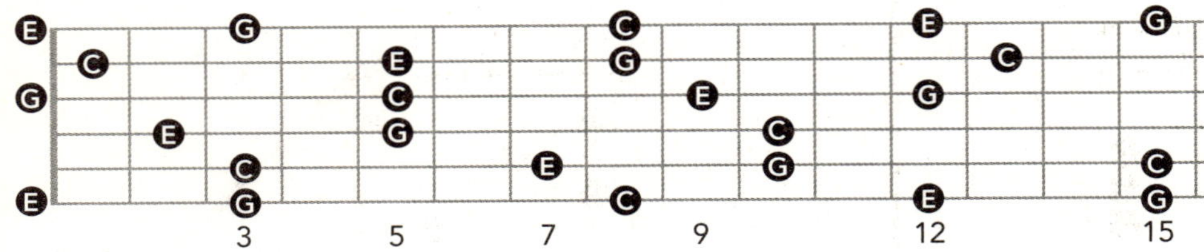

4) Look at these notes carefully—familiar open chord shapes will start to appear.

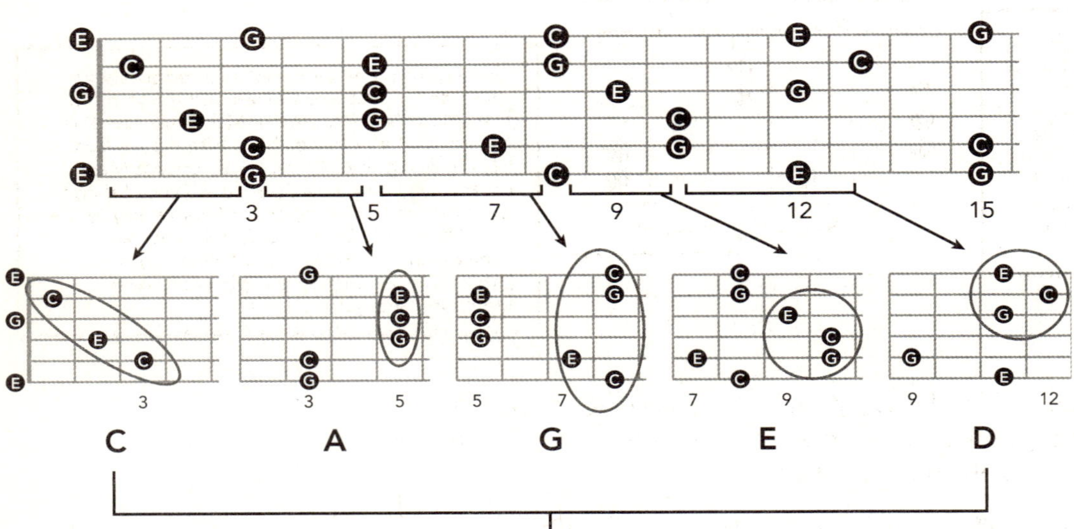

And here they are: the common C, A, G, E, and D chord shapes. Keep in mind these don't necessarily represent the actual names of the chords. Instead, they represent the five positions of a single major chord (in this case, C Major) as it appears across the entire fretboard. By shifting this pattern up and down the neck, you can now use familiar open chord shapes to play any major chord, in any position.

Lesson 4: Simplifying the CAGED System

You might be wondering: is there a way to simplify the CAGED system to make it easier to visualize? Well, there is an alternate, and perhaps easier, way. Rather than conceptualize five chord shapes connected across the entire fretboard, you might try to visualize four chord shapes that are connected to two root locations. One of the roots is on the 5th string (A), and the other is on the 6th string (low E). Visualizing these two roots as a "toggle switch" with a chord on each side is a very practical way to simplify these patterns; especially since chord shape 2 and 4 are common barre chords. Study the following diagram carefully to understand this concept.

Start off with the CAGED system, using the C Major chord:

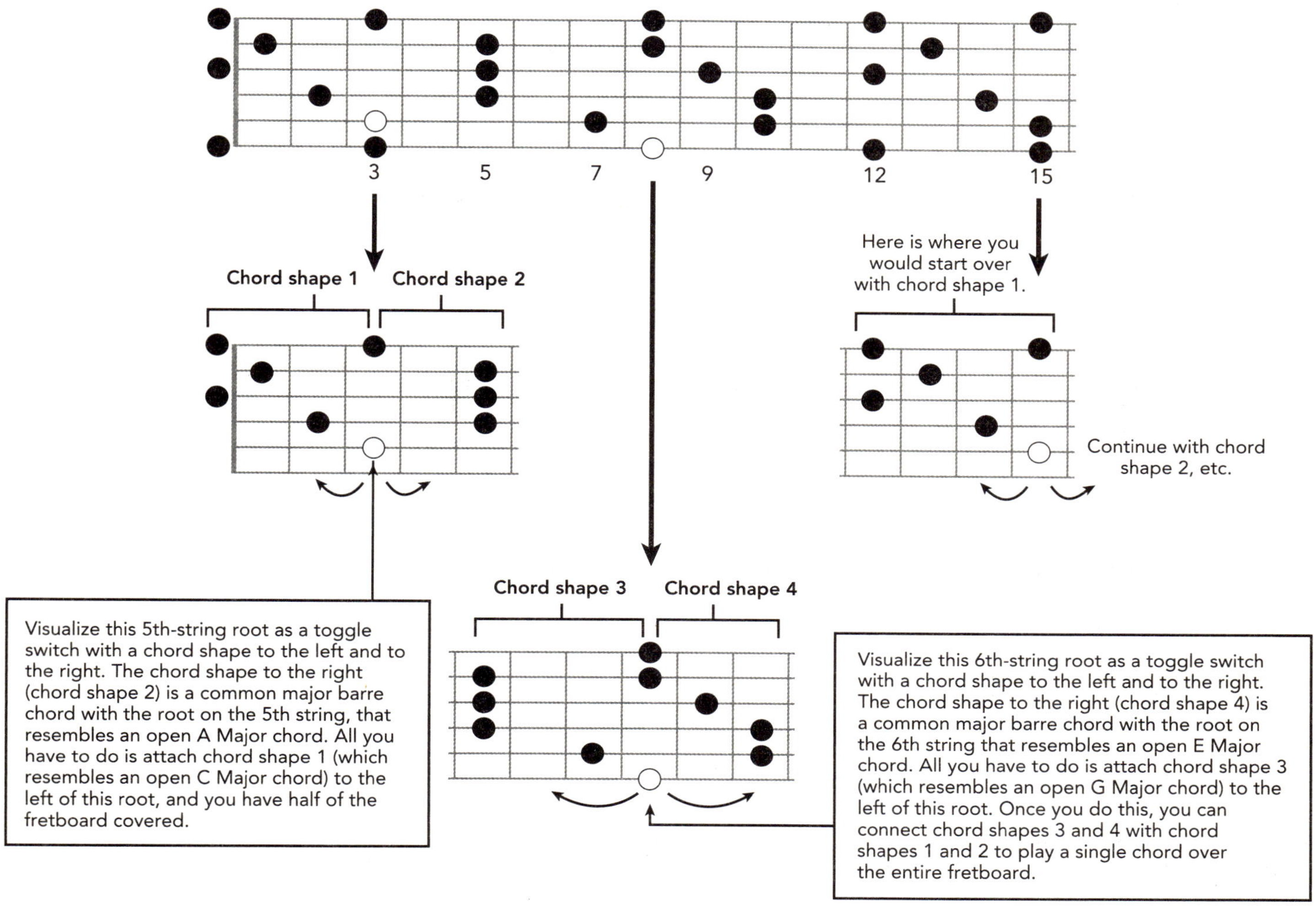

Chord shape 1   **Chord shape 2**

Here is where you would start over with chord shape 1.

Continue with chord shape 2, etc.

Chord shape 3   **Chord shape 4**

Visualize this 5th-string root as a toggle switch with a chord shape to the left and to the right. The chord shape to the right (chord shape 2) is a common major barre chord with the root on the 5th string, that resembles an open A Major chord. All you have to do is attach chord shape 1 (which resembles an open C Major chord) to the left of this root, and you have half of the fretboard covered.

Visualize this 6th-string root as a toggle switch with a chord shape to the left and to the right. The chord shape to the right (chord shape 4) is a common major barre chord with the root on the 6th string that resembles an open E Major chord. All you have to do is attach chord shape 3 (which resembles an open G Major chord) to the left of this root. Once you do this, you can connect chord shapes 3 and 4 with chord shapes 1 and 2 to play a single chord over the entire fretboard.

Now remember, this entire system is movable. So, if you were going to apply the CAGED system to, say, a G♯ Major chord, you would shift the entire system down four frets so that the root was G♯. The pattern would now look like this:

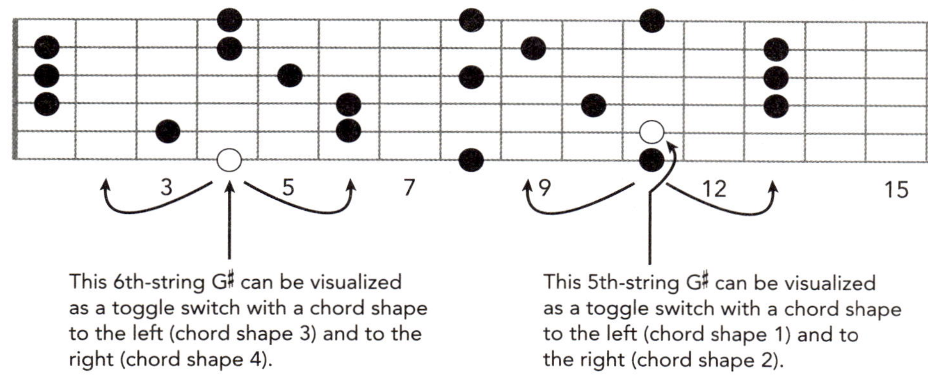

This 6th-string G♯ can be visualized as a toggle switch with a chord shape to the left (chord shape 3) and to the right (chord shape 4).

This 5th-string G♯ can be visualized as a toggle switch with a chord shape to the left (chord shape 1) and to the right (chord shape 2).

Lesson 5: Movable Fretboard Shapes

Visualizing chords and scales as movable shapes offers incredible bang-for-your-buck potential; every shape that exists on the fretboard can be relocated to all 12 keys without altering its visual appearance. So, when you learn new chords and scales on the guitar, it's important to realize how much you are really learning. Read on for some prime examples of how well this approach works.

How to turn four chord shapes into 48 chords in no time:

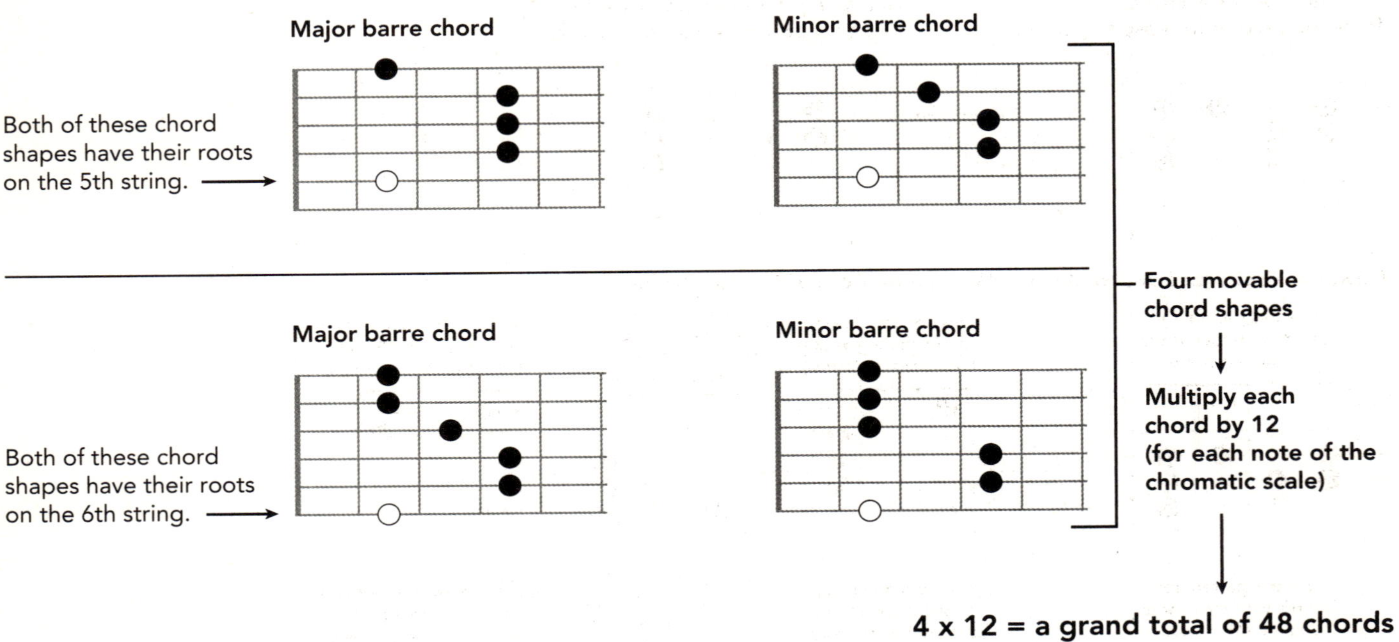

The term *pentatonic scale* applies to any five-note scale. However, the term is almost always used in reference to one of two specific types of pentatonic scales: the *minor pentatonic scale* or the *major pentatonic scale*. Luckily, as the diagrams to the right illustrate, both scales can be constructed from the same scale shape. To build the desired scale, just make sure you know where to visualize the root, or tonal center.

How to turn two pentatonic scale shapes into 48 scales in no time:

This pentatonic scale shape can be associated with two tonal centers, both of which are located on the 5th string. ⟶

Use this note as your tonal center to get a minor pentatonic scale.

Use this note as your tonal center to get a major pentatonic scale.

This pentatonic scale shape can be associated with two tonal centers, both of which are located on the 6th string. ⟶

Use this note as your tonal center to get a minor pentatonic scale.

Use this note as your tonal center to get a major pentatonic scale.

Four movable pentatonic scale shapes

Multiply times 12 (for each note of the chromatic scale)

4 x 12 = a grand total of 48 scales

Lesson 6: Using Scale Degrees to Build Chords

1) Start off with a one-octave major scale on one string.

2) Arrange the notes into a four-fret pattern for easy fingering.

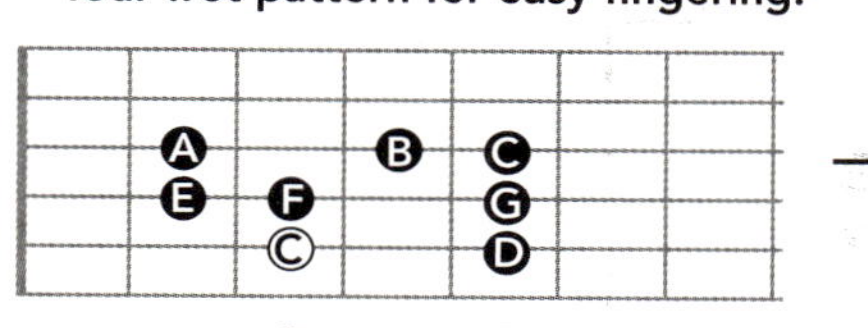

3) Replace the note names with their appropriate scale degrees.

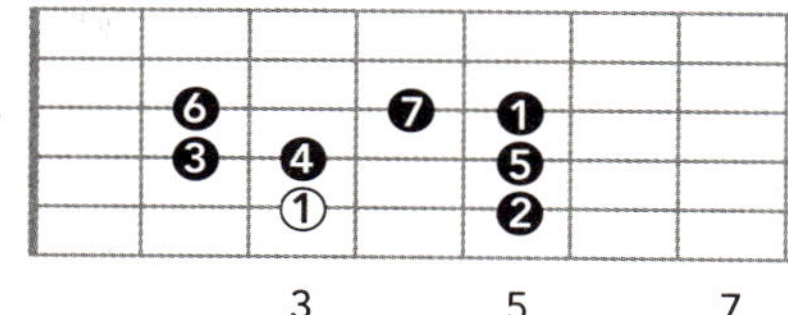

4) Now, use the major scale to identify the scale degrees of familiar chords.

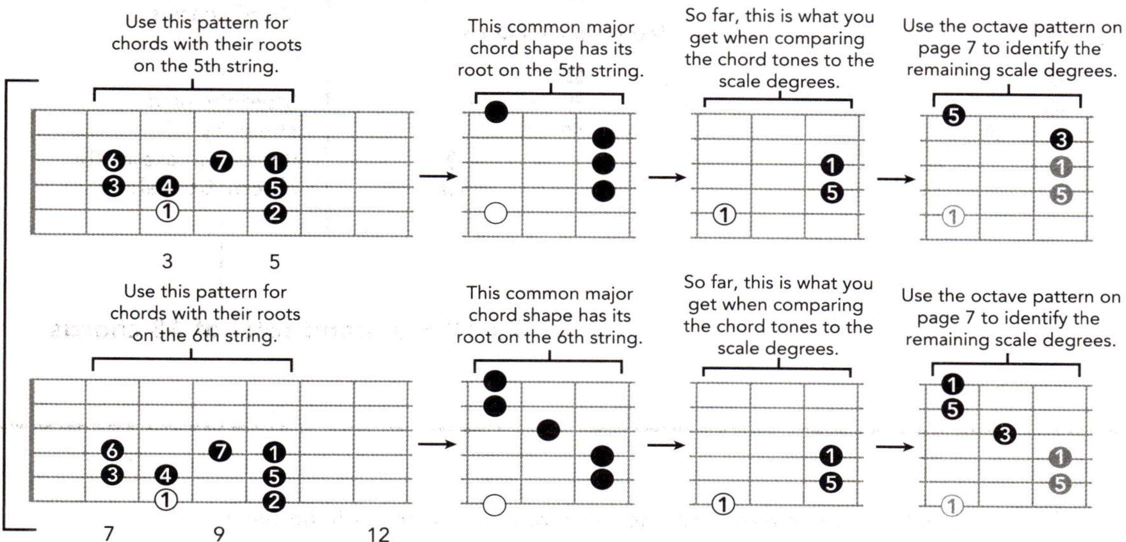

5) Now that the chord tones are identified as scale degrees, alter them to create new chords.

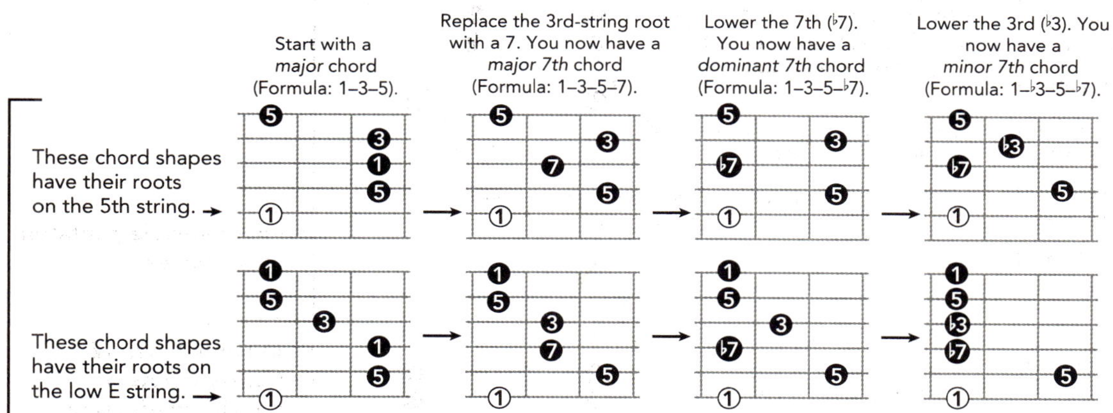

6) Let's do the math on the example above. We took two chord voicings (step 4 above) and turned them into eight voicings (step 5 above) by adding only three new chord formulas. Now, multiply all eight chords shown above by 12 (for each note in the chromatic scale): **8 x 12 = a grand total of 96 chords.**

As you can see, this chapter contains an enormous amount of material. It is important to take your time absorbing these concepts as you enjoy making music with the chapters that follow. Remember, it's not *what* you know that will get you far, but rather how much you can *do* with what you know. With this in mind, head to the next chapter and get ready for some music.

+ +

Lesson 1: Palm Muting

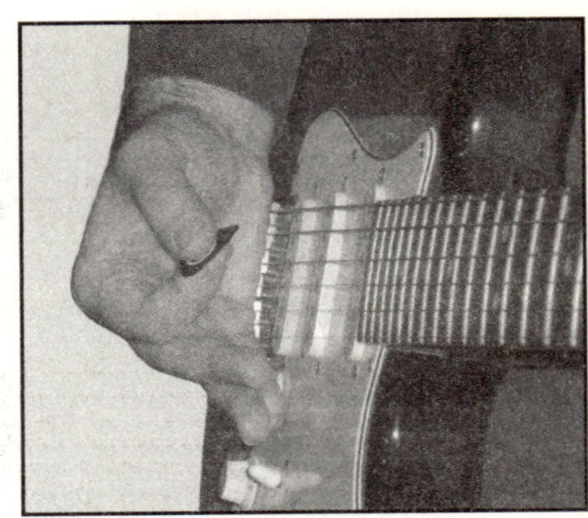

Palm mute.

It could be argued that one of the most important elements of rock music is *distortion*. Whether you get your distortion from an overdriven amp or from stepping on a pedal, when you combine distortion with a *palm mute*, you get the traditional heavy rock sound.

While holding the pick between your thumb and index finger, build the palm mute by placing the side of your palm partially on the strings and partially on the bridge, as shown in the photo. Set your tone for a thick overdriven sound. Then, play the following exercise with palm-muted downstrokes for an extra chunky crunch.

P.M. = Palm mute.

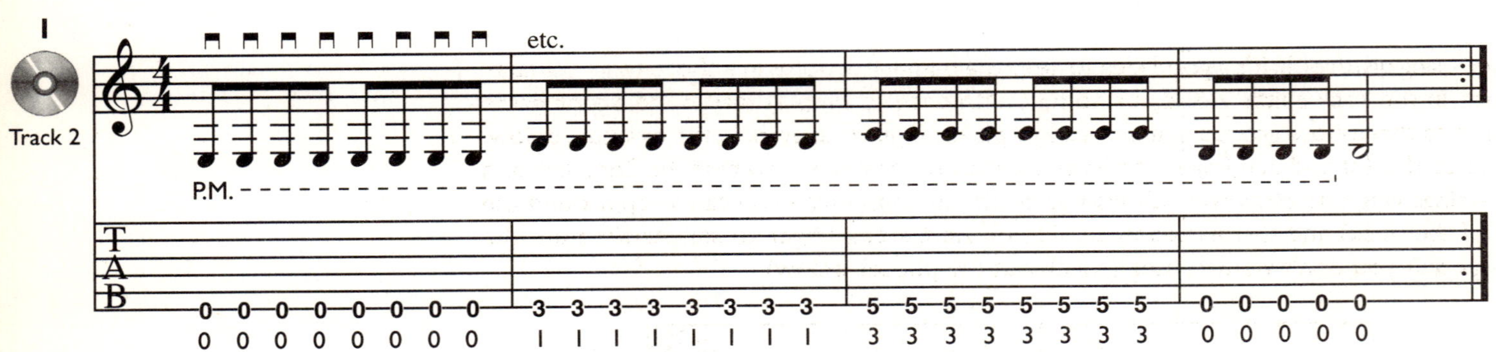

A very effective device in the rock guitar world is to mix palm muting with strummed chords. In the next example, check out how we create rhythmic punctuation by bouncing between palm mutes on the 5th and 6th strings, and strums on the middle strings. The rhythmic variety is limitless when you mix and match strumming techniques.

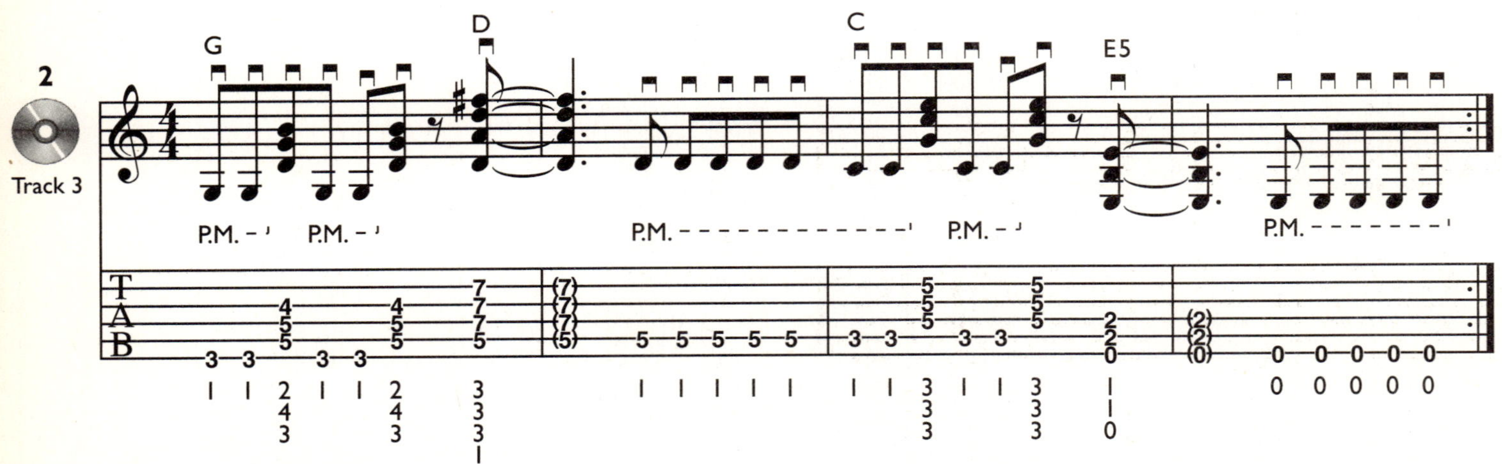

Lesson 2: Rock Chords

Distortion can make everyday chords sound powerful. However, it's worth noting that some of the most massive-sounding chords are often constructed from only a few chord tones. The most common are *power chords* or *5 chords*, built from the root and 5th (and sometimes the octave). Since power chords are built from such an economy of notes, the result is a tone that's tight, focused, and crunchy. As you check out the two- and three-note power chord variations in the next example, notice how you can drastically alter the tone of each chord by engaging and disengaging the palm mute.

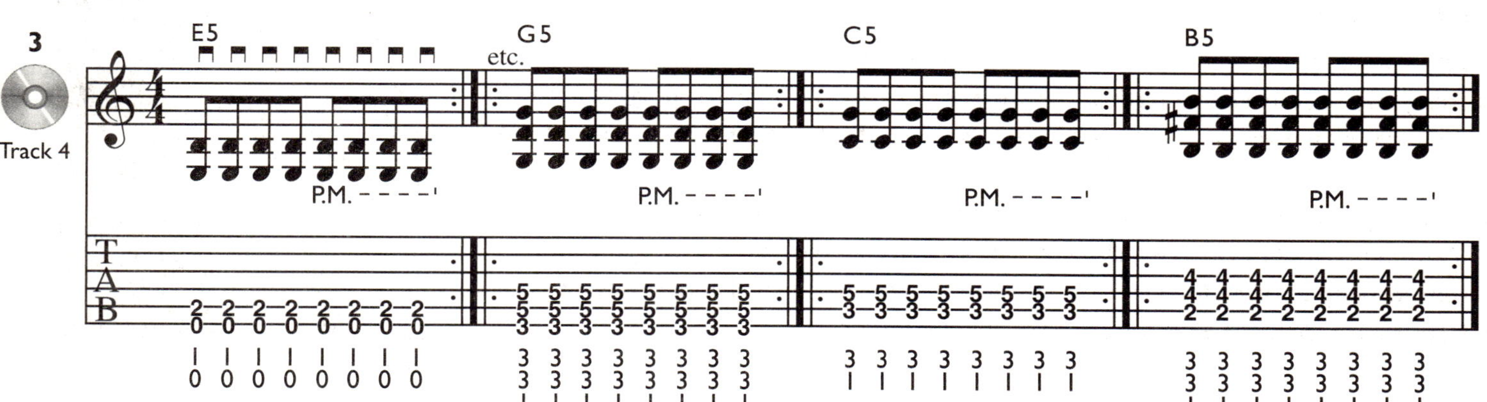

When using distortion, it's a good idea to keep the number of notes in a chord to a minimum. In fact, in the rock guitar world, it's common practice to simplify major and minor barre chords to three-note groups that are easy to play and quick to grab. In the example below, it's up to the 1st and 3rd fingers to flatten across the fretboard so that the 2nd, 3rd, and 4th strings ring out. However, it's also up to the thumb (which you can wrap around the top of the neck) and the arched underside of the fretting finger to selectively mute the strings that you don't want to ring (check out the photos below).

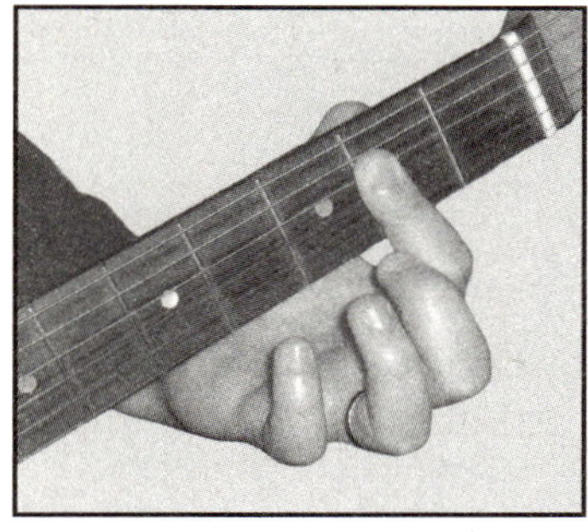

1st-finger barre.

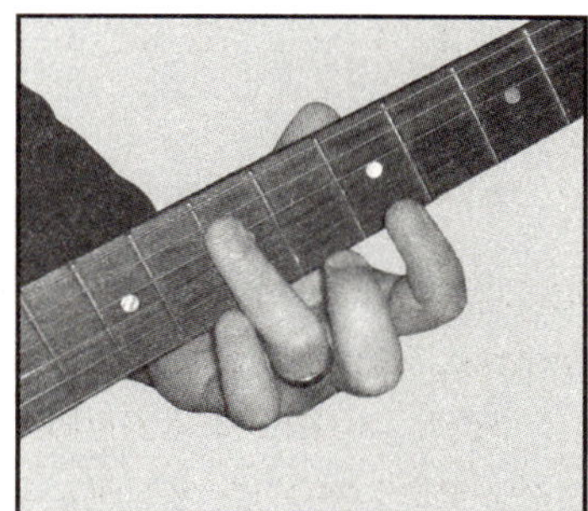

3rd-finger barre.

Now, let's take the palm muting technique we looked at in Lesson 1 and mix it together with the power chord and one-finger barre techniques we looked at in Lesson 2. Below is a tune in the style of "Rockin' in the Free World" by Neil Young that features all of these skills. It also uses the *hammer-on* technique, which is performed by playing the first note normally, then hammering a left-hand finger onto the fretboard to sound a second note without picking with your right hand.

Muting and Barring on the Fretboard

Track 6

Lesson 3: Rock Chord Shapes

This lesson deals with some of the special chord voicings rock guitarists use. The good news is that these chord voicings are designed to be very easy to finger, which facilitates switching from chord to chord quickly and comfortably. In addition, these special chord shapes all relate to the larger CAGED system covered on page 8.

Speaking of which, take a close look at the C, A, and E shapes from the CAGED system below. Notice how these three larger shapes can be simplified to form three- and four-note voicings. Give these chord shapes a try with plenty of overdrive, and you'll be rockin' in no time.

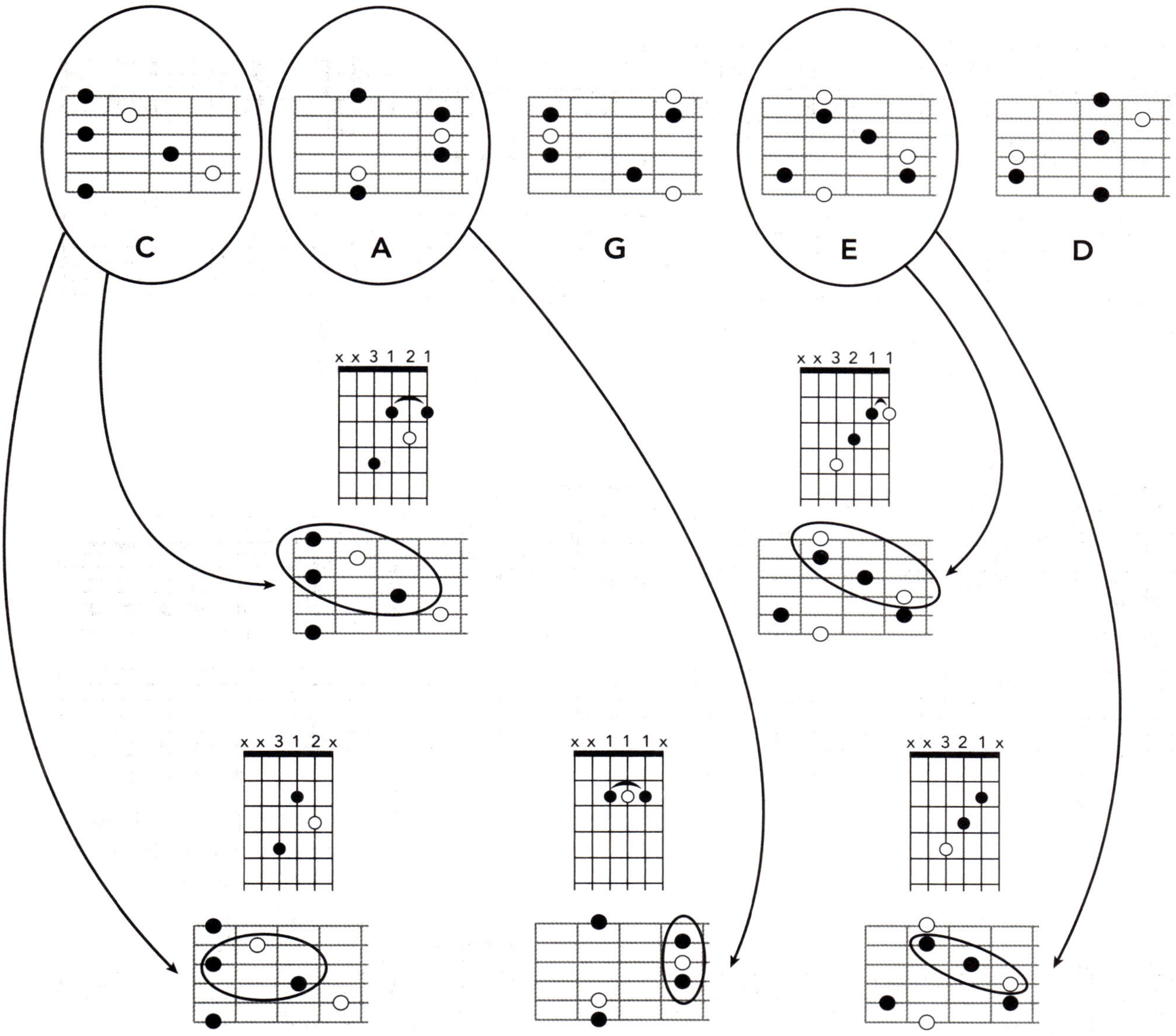

Lesson 4: Rock Chord Progressions

Now, let's put these chord voicings to work. The next example uses two chord shapes that are strung together in a descending sequence. As you play through these chords, notice how each voicing moves a very small distance when switching to the next chord. This concept is called *smooth voice leading*.

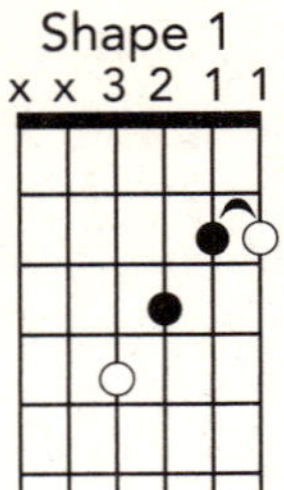

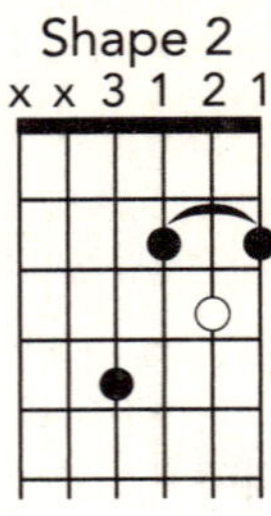

Voice-Leading Labyrinth

Track 7

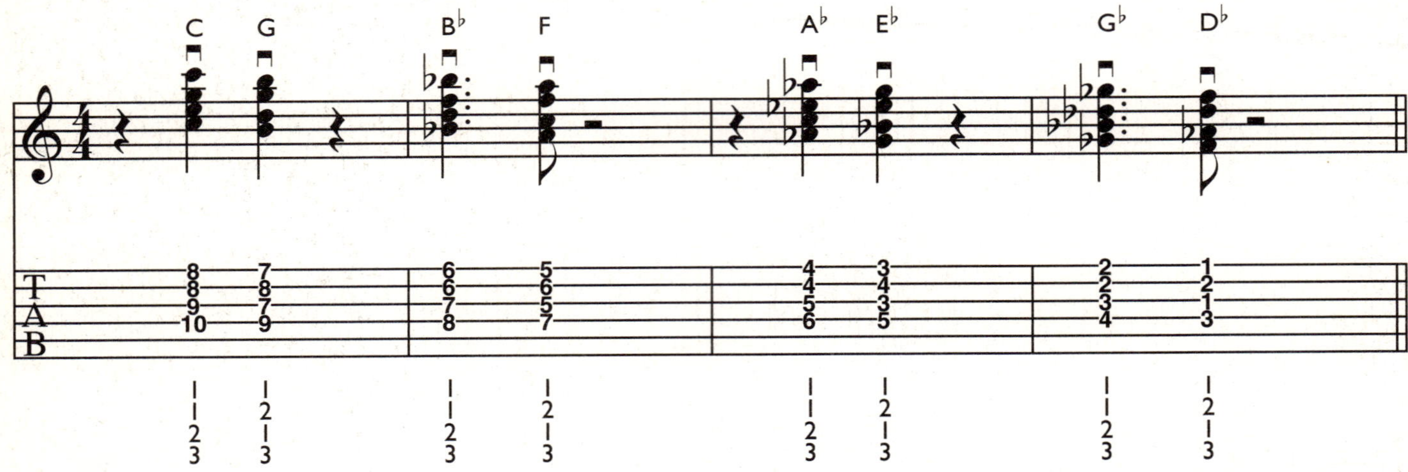

Speaking of smooth voice leading, take a look at the next example. These three voicings are so close together that they even share some common tones. Also, watch out for the last measure on this one—it's a quick switch.

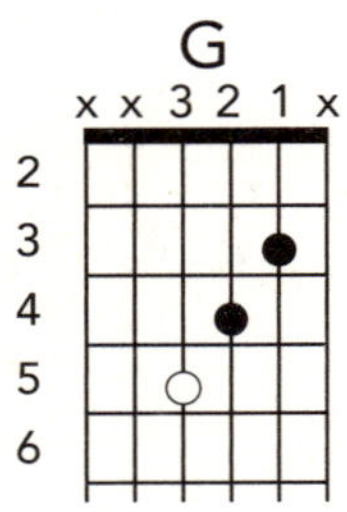

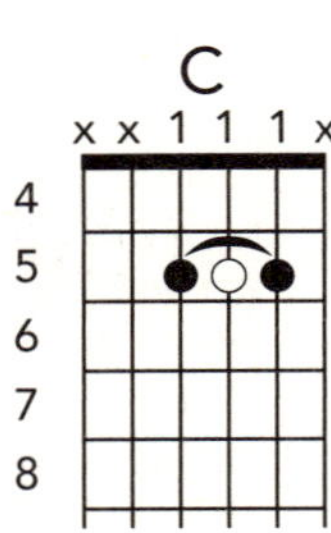

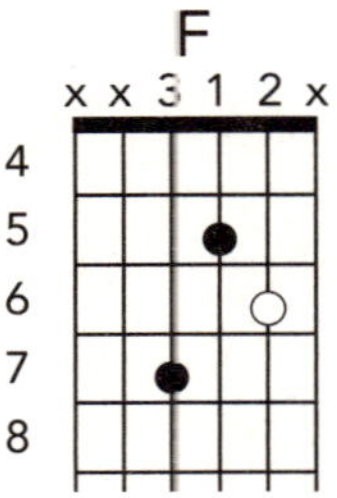

Three-String Strum

Track 8

     The Guitar Style Resource

Here is a song in the style of "Brown Sugar" by the Rolling Stones. This tune features all of the rock chord voicings that were covered in this lesson, plus a few extras.

Sweet Molasses

Track 9

Lesson 5: Rock Chord Embellishments

Now, let's add *embellishments* to some of the chords we've been working on. Embellishments are usually made up of neighboring scale tones directly above and below the tones of the chord, and they are often played with hammer-ons and *pull-offs* (see page 22). Jimi Hendrix was a true master of this technique. See if you can hear some of his influence in the examples below. On the CD, the examples are joined together and played straight through.

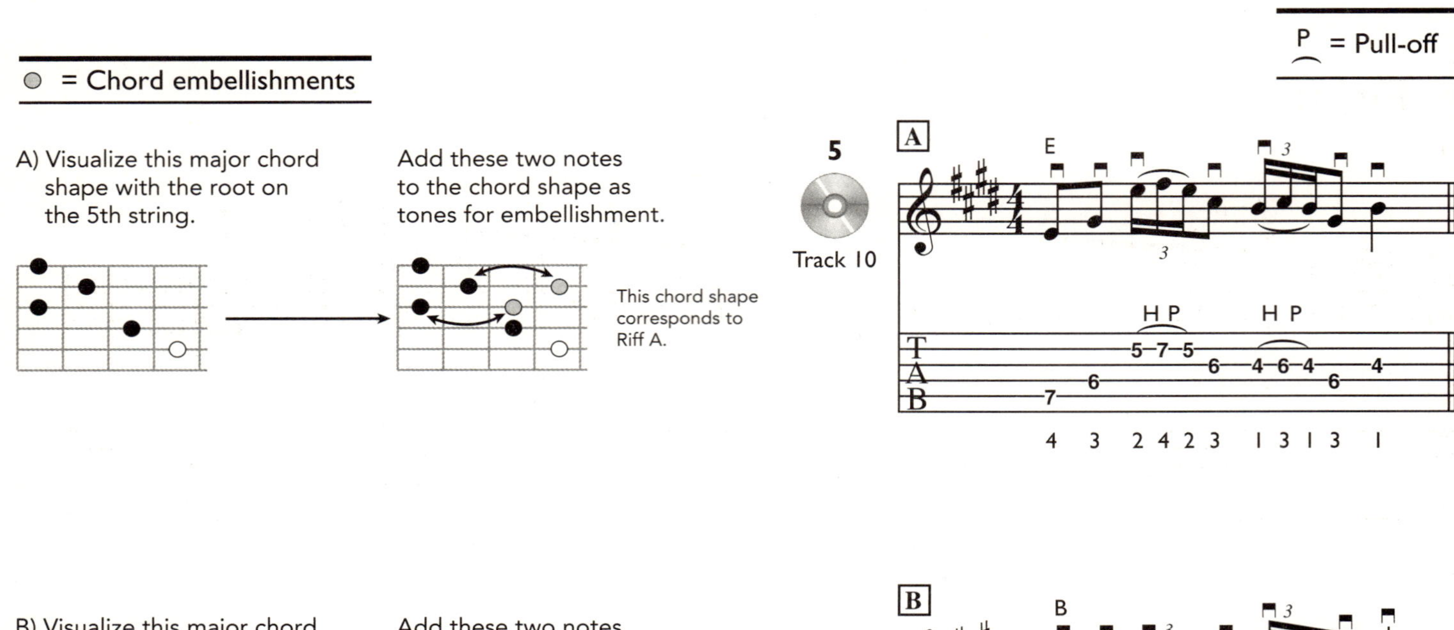

A) Visualize this major chord shape with the root on the 5th string.

Add these two notes to the chord shape as tones for embellishment.

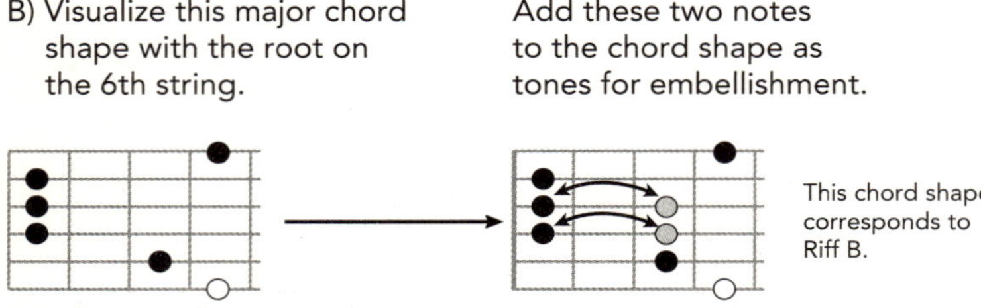

This chord shape corresponds to Riff A.

B) Visualize this major chord shape with the root on the 6th string.

Add these two notes to the chord shape as tones for embellishment.

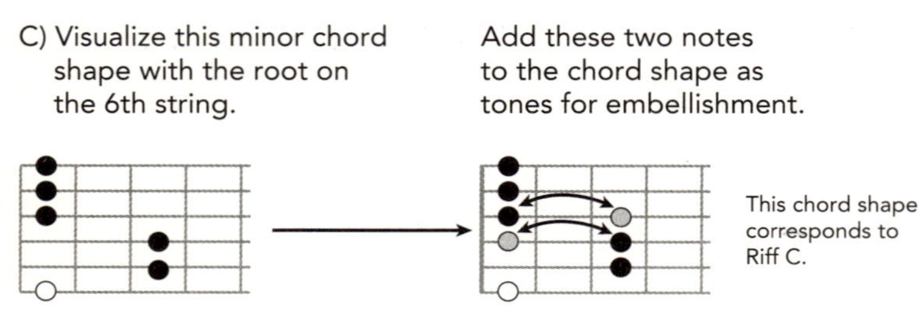

This chord shape corresponds to Riff B.

C) Visualize this minor chord shape with the root on the 6th string.

Add these two notes to the chord shape as tones for embellishment.

This chord shape corresponds to Riff C.

The next step with these chord embellishments is to add *double stops*. Double stops occur when two strings are picked simultaneously. After a double stop is plucked, typically, one string is sustained while the other string is embellished with hammer-ons and pull-offs. Hendrix's genius with double stops and chord embellishments has influenced countless guitarists, including John Frusciante of The Red Hot Chili Peppers. To see how this technique can be used in a song, check out the example below; it's in the style of "Snow" by The Red Hot Chili Peppers.

Frost

Track 11

Looking for more notes to embellish your chords? Well, here is a trick that will help you become a truly versatile guitarist. Combine the chord shapes below with their respective chord embellishments, and then superimpose the resulting notes on top of one another. The result is the same collection of notes. Take a look at these diagrams to visualize how this works:

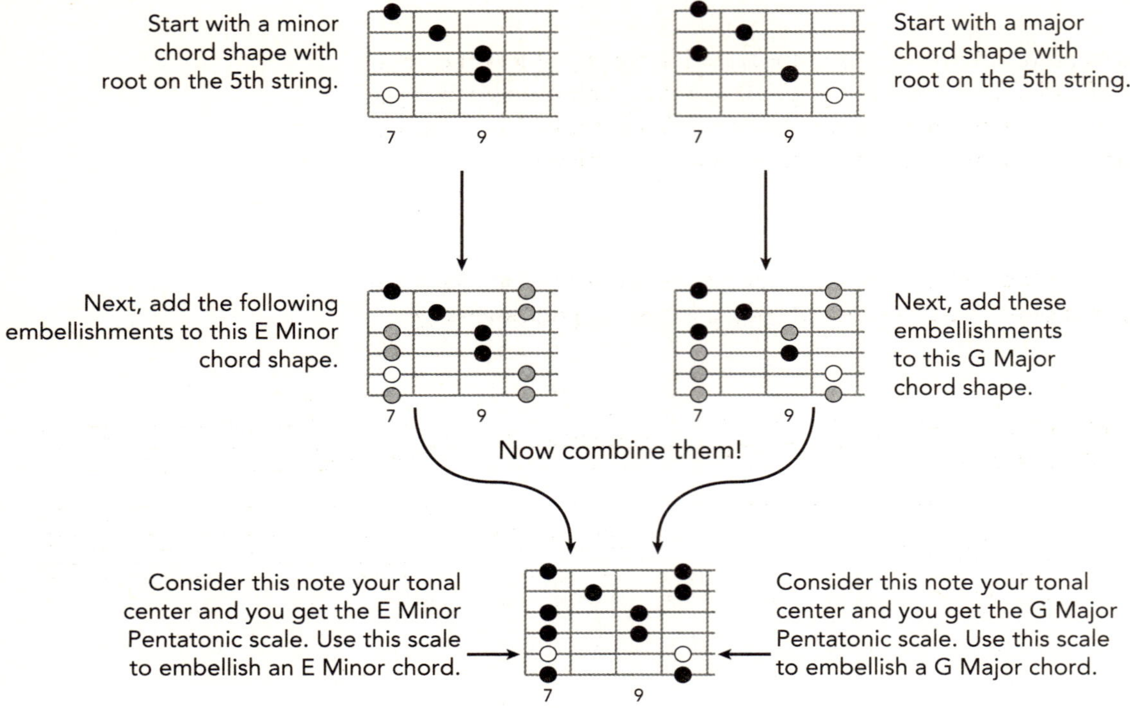

Now, let's do the same thing with minor and major chords that have their roots on the 6th string.

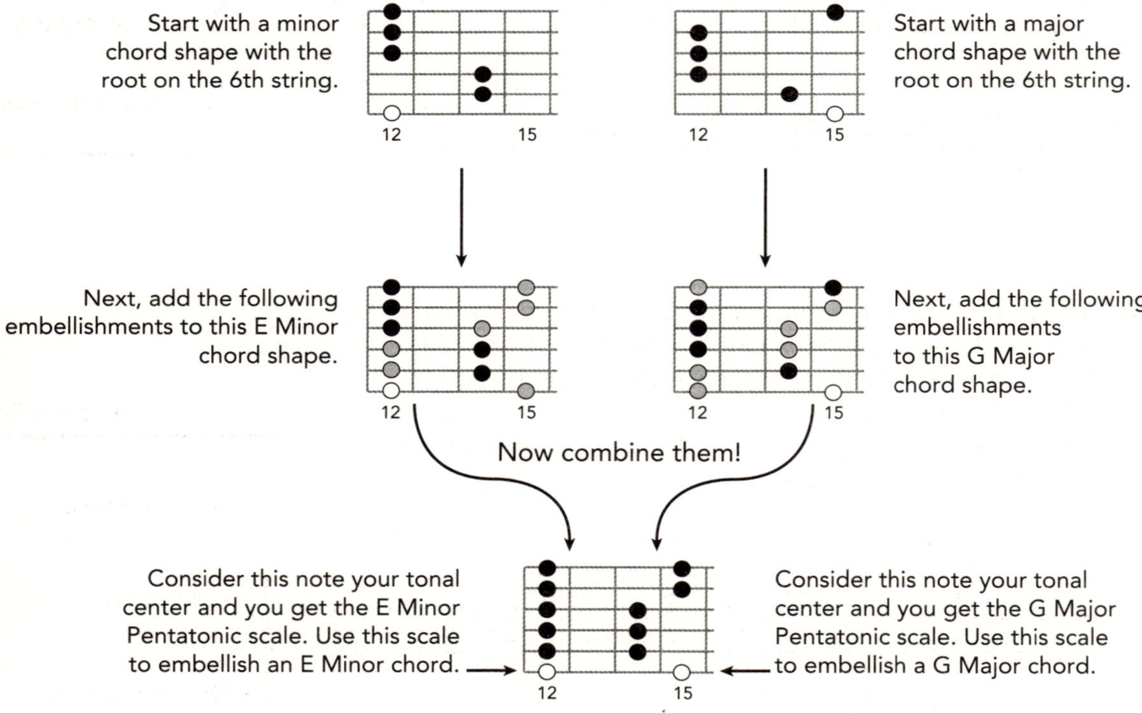

The goal of this approach is to visualize your chords, chord embellishments, and scales as separate, yet connected entities. Imagine the possibilities.

Lesson 6: Soloing in a Rock Style

Following are some solo licks written in a rock style. Tone-wise, these phrases will sound great with distortion and an aggressive pick attack. In addition, you might try playing these licks with your pickup selector switched to your bridge (or treble) pickup in order to help your "axe" cut through the mix.

For fun, try to play these solo patterns over the rock tunes in this chapter. All of the licks in this lesson are in the key of E Minor, which will work perfectly over "Muting and Barring on the Fretboard" (page 14), which is also in the key of E Minor. To get these licks to work over "Frost" (page 19), transpose them up four frets to the key of G# Minor.

Alternate Picking

Alternate picking involves moving the pick up and down in a continuous fashion. Because of the economy of motion, it is often the technique of choice for picking quick passages.

Slides

Sliding is a crucial rock technique that is achieved by following these steps: After picking a fretted note, slide the fretting finger up or down to another note. Keep moderate pressure on the note while sliding, and an ascending or descending pitch will be produced.

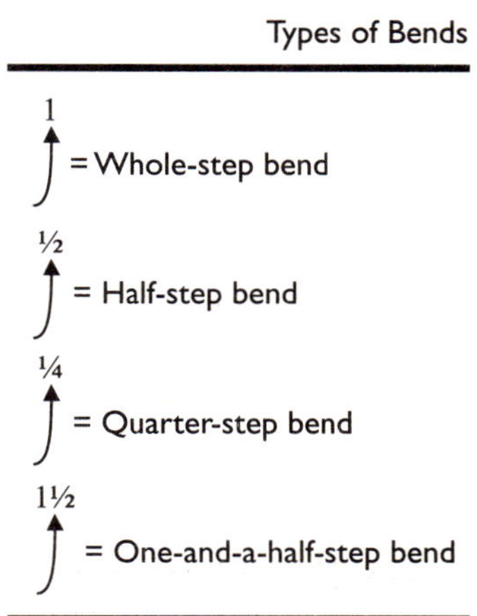

Double-Stop Bends

The next lick features a classic rock technique that's been used in countless guitar solos. In this *double-stop bend* example, the 1st and 3rd fingers of the left hand are placed on the 2nd and 3rd strings, which are plucked simultaneously. As the notes ring, the 3rd finger bends the note on the 3rd string toward the middle of the fretboard, while the 1st finger holds the note on the 2nd string steady. Ever hear the saying "two notes are better than one?" With this riff, two notes *become* one.

Types of Bends

Pull-Offs

A *pull-off* is produced when the finger holding a fretted note is "snapped" off of the fretboard to another fretted note or open string fast enough to set the string in motion. In this example, plant your 1st, 2nd, and 4th fingers on the appropriate notes. Once all three fingers are placed and the first note is picked, the 4th finger snaps off to the 2nd finger, then the 2nd finger snaps off to the 1st finger. You get two consecutive pull-offs from one pick attack.

Hammer-Ons

A *hammer-on* is the direct opposite of a pull-off. Instead of snapping the left-hand finger *off* of the string, this technique involves *hammering* a left-hand finger *on* to the fretboard, setting the string in motion. This example demonstrates how to quickly ascend through a minor pentatonic scale by way of hammer-ons.

Hammer-Ons, Pull-Offs, and Bends

The example below demonstrates how hammer-ons, pull-offs, and bends can be combined to create awesome rock licks. Make sure to start off slow and play through this lick many times, gradually picking up speed (this goes for the other riffs as well). With practice, you'll be using these techniques in your own rock solos in no time.

CHAPTER THREE
BLUES GUITAR

+ +

Lesson 1: Roman Numerals

Undoubtedly, the blues is one of the most influential styles of music in recent history. In fact, the blues laid the groundwork for entire genres of music, like rock, jazz, pop, and more. Since it's at the heart of so many styles of music, getting familiar with the blues is extremely important. Plus, it's a blast to play.

It's important to note that musicians often look at chord progressions as a sequence of Roman numerals. This is a very powerful system of *harmonic analysis* that describes chords in terms of how they function in relation to the key of a song (or section of music). You can use this system to rationalize chords that are *diatonic* (within the key) and chords that are *non-diatonic* (outside of the key). Here's how the Roman numeral system works:

Roman Numerals	
I or i	1
II or ii	2
III or iii	3
IV or iv	4
V or v	5
VI or vi	6
VII or vii	7

Step 1) To identify the diatonic chords in the key of C, you will need to construct a C Major scale. On paper, this is done by lining up the notes C, D, E, F, G, A, B, and C on a treble clef staff. (To construct the major scale on the fretboard, refer to pages 5, 10, and 92.)

Step 2) Place an E and a G on top of the first note of the C Major scale, creating a "stack" of notes that spell C, E, and G from low to high. This creates a C chord built upon the first note of the scale. Then, using diatonic notes from the scale, build a similar stack on top of each note in the scale. This produces a harmonized major scale and gives us the diatonic chords in the key of C.

Step 3) Turn the chord progression into a sequence of Roman numerals. You now have all of the diatonic triads in the key of C. Note that the major chords use upper-case Roman numerals while the minor and diminished (dim or ○) chords use lower-case.

So, if you were to switch to the key of A, the roots of the sequence of chords would change, but the Roman numerals would stay the same. For example, here are the diatonic triads in the key of A:

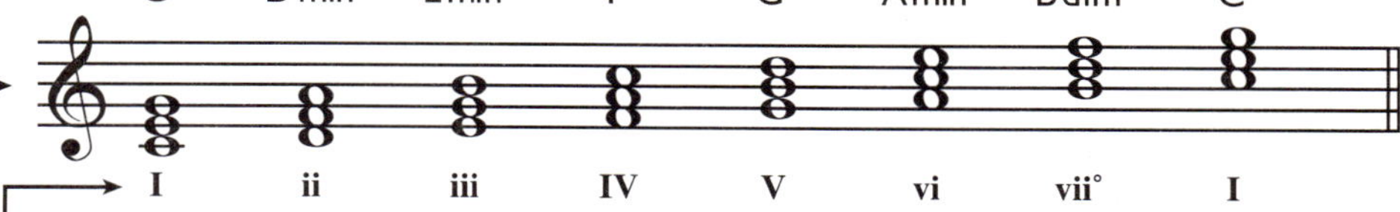

I	ii	iii	IV	V	vi	vii°	I
A	Bmin	C#min	D	E	F#min	G#dim	A

The most common chords found in the blues are the I, IV, and V chords. This means in the key of C, you would end up with a C chord (the I chord), an F chord (the IV chord), and a G chord (the V chord). It's also common practice for blues players to spice these chords up by turning them into dominant 7th chords. Simply tack the new chord quality onto the same Roman numerals and you get a I7–IV7–V7 chord progression.

Lesson 2: The 12-Bar Blues

Now, we are ready to look at the most common form for this genre, the *12-bar blues*. Even though there are a ton of harmonic variations for the 12-bar blues, we'll look at the most common form. Start with the I7 chord in bar 1; switch to the IV7 in bar 2 (this is known as a *quick four*); return to the I7 for bars 3–4; play the IV7 in bars 5–6; return to the I7 in bars 7–8; play the V7 in bar 9; the IV7 in bar 10; return to the I7 chord for measures 11–12. Keeping these guidelines in mind, here is a 12-bar blues in the key of C along with some choice dominant 7th voicings for you to use (at the bottom of the page).

Basic 12-Bar Blues

Track 13

Using the three voicings below, you can play through the progression above without even switching position.

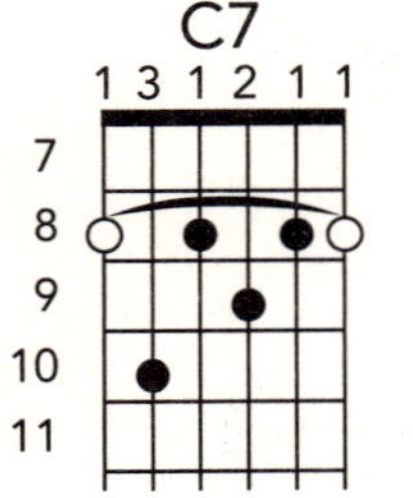

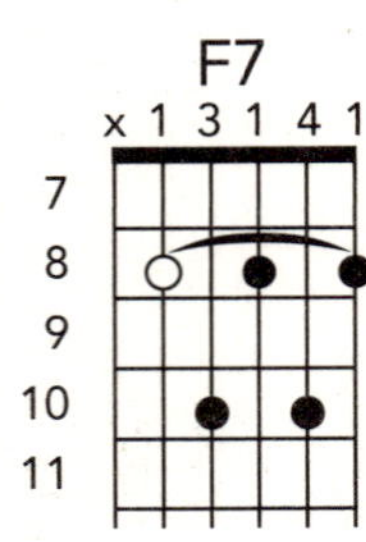

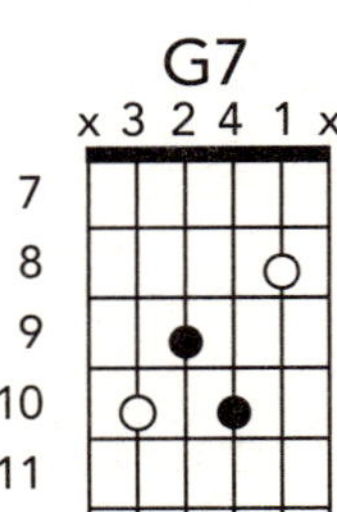

The example below is a 12-bar blues in the style of the famous tune "The Thrill Is Gone," popularized by B. B. King. There are two significant differences between this 12-bar blues and the basic 12-bar blues example on the previous page. First, this is an A Minor blues. This means the "one" and "four" chords are both minor chords instead of dominant 7th chords.

The other difference has to do with the 9th bar, which is where we would normally find the V chord. In this case, the V chord (E) has been pushed to the 10th bar. So, what's in the 9th bar? Well, it's an F chord. To give the F chord an appropriate Roman numeral, it's important to realize that the Roman numeral system (which is based on the major scale) can be altered with sharps and flats to accommodate the roots of non-diatonic chords.

So, by realizing that the F chord is a half-step lower than the diatonic vi chord in the key of A (which would be an F♯min chord), you could now "flat" the diatonic vi chord by a half-step (down to F) and make it a major chord instead of a minor chord. The F chord is a ♭VI chord in the key of A Minor. Now that we have looked at the chord progression, let's check out this awesome minor blues.

The Chile's Gone

Track 14

♪ = *Staccato.* Play this note short and detached

Lesson 3: The Blues Shuffle

A key aspect of the blues that every guitarist should be acquainted with is the *shuffle*. The blues shuffle is a specific rhythm feel characterized by a long, accented pulse followed by a shorter, weaker pulse. In rhythmic terms, it could be approximated as a *triplet* (three eighth notes in the space of one beat) with the first two eighth notes tied.

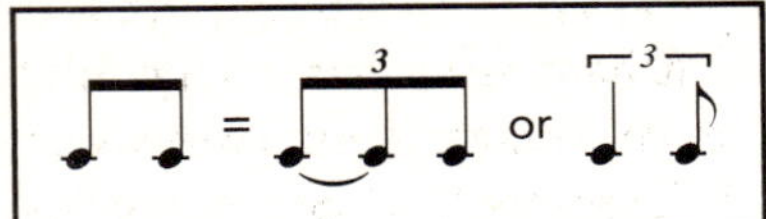

The tune below features a shuffle feel in a medium-tempo blues. It's in the style of a classic tune called "Worried Life Blues" recorded by Big Maceo Merriweather in 1941. This 8-bar blues has gone on to become a staple of the blues repertoire, and has since been covered by artists like John Lee Hooker and Eric Clapton. There are a few important features worth pointing out:

1) It's not a 12-bar blues. Instead, it's an 8-bar form.

2) It contains something known as a *turnaround*. In the blues, a turnaround is a short, catchy melodic phrase designed to get you from the last one or two bars of the tune back to the beginning of the form.

3) The last chord of the first ending is a G Augmented chord (abbreviated Gaug or G+). This type of chord is sometimes used as a spicy V chord substitute that sounds great when it resolves to the I chord (at the beginning of the form).

The Troubled 8-Bar Shuffle

Track 15

     The Guitar Style Resource

There are a number of common variations you'll find with the blues shuffle. In the spirit of variety and versatility, here are some other patterns for you to try. However, get ready for a left-hand workout; it's the 4th finger that does most of the action with these variations. Also, even though these patterns are all riffs over a single C chord, they can be applied to the I, IV, and the V chord in any key. Give it a try. Remember, the shuffle has a "swing feel," and this is usually written as regular eighth notes. For the remainder of this book, the swing rhythm is indicated at the beginning of each piece with: *Swing 8ths*.

Shuffle Patterns

Here is a quick-tempo blues shuffle in the style of the Stevie Ray Vaughan masterpiece "Pride and Joy." As you play through this example, take special note of the alternate picking pattern, which should facilitate playing at a fast tempo. Also, you may want to experiment with flattening out extraneous fingers in your fretting hand to selectively mute strings that you don't want to be played. This way, you can make wider, more rhythmically percussive alternate strokes, and only the note that you are fretting will ring out. This example also features a classic turnaround.

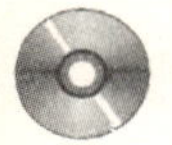

Stevie's Shuffle

Track 17

     The Guitar Style Resource

Lesson 4: The $\frac{12}{8}$ Blues

The most common meter for the slow blues is $\frac{12}{8}$, and it is a close relative to the shuffle. But before playing through a $\frac{12}{8}$ example, let's take a look at a few new movable chord voicings and check out a new barre technique for fingering some of these spicy chords.

This G9 shape is a blues chord that is great to know. You can use this voicing in place of any regular major triad or dominant 7th chord.

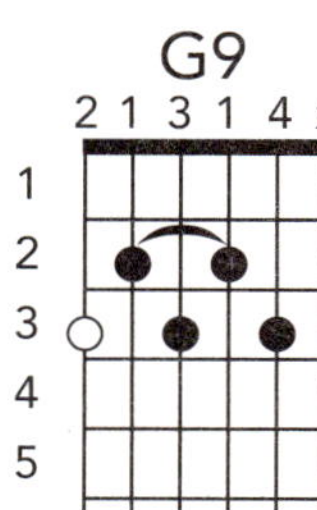

Often, when this chord is used, it is accompanied by, or even replaced by, this classic sliding riff:

This C9 chord is equivalent to the G9 voicing above, but the root is on the A string.

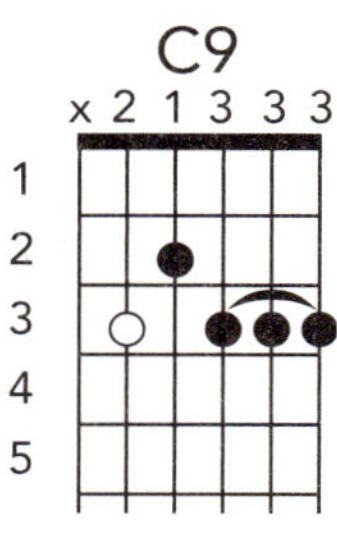

Building this chord requires a special technique that involves flattening out the 3rd finger, as shown in the photo to the right:

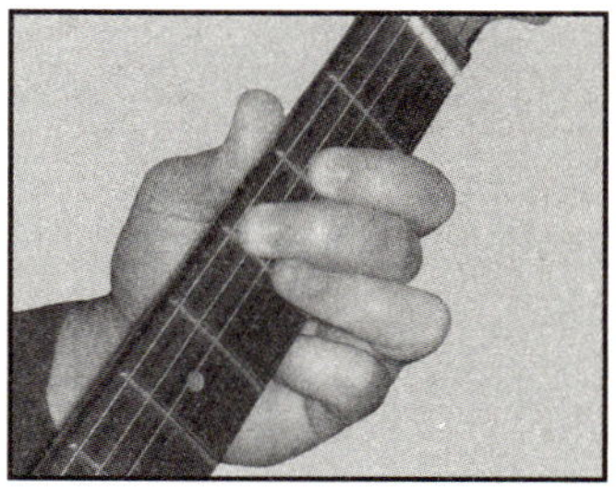

The C9 chord.

One way to spice up an average minor chord with the root on the 5th string is to turn it into a minor 7 chord like this:

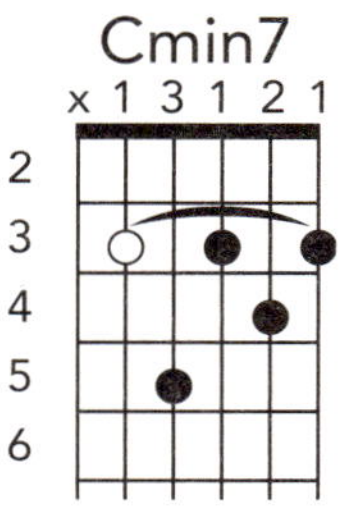

Once you can comfortably form this voicing, try sliding your 3rd finger to create a phrase similar to the G9 riff above:

Use this minor 7 voicing to spice up a minor chord with the root on the 6th string.

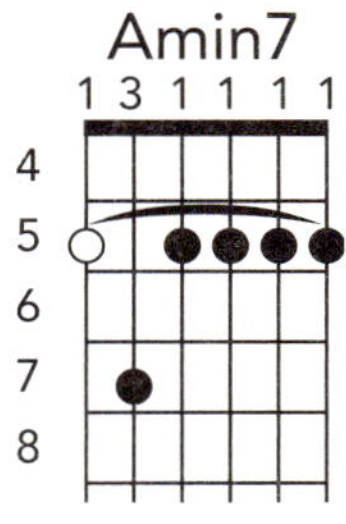

Here is an alternate way to finger a minor 7 chord with the root on the 6th string. It uses the same 3rd finger barre technique that was used on the C9 voicing above. Take a look at the photo to the right for correct finger placement.

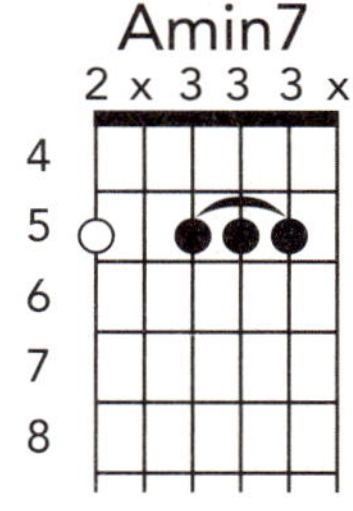

This special voicing is legendary. Known as the *Hendrix chord*, it's especially effective as a V chord voicing. It sounds great on the last bar of a blues progression.

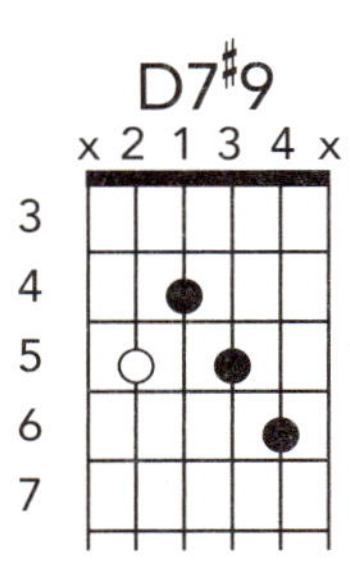

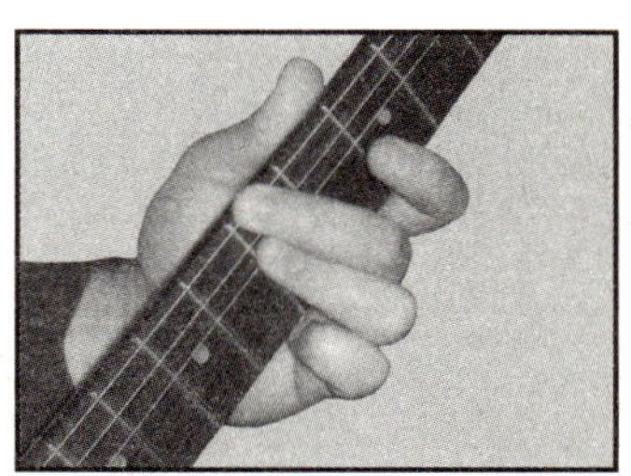

The Amin7 chord.

Now that we have a bunch of new blues voicings to work with, let's put them to use in a $\frac{12}{8}$ blues. This tune below is a 12-bar slow blues in the style of "Stormy Monday" by the legendary T-Bone Walker. T-Bone originally recorded the tune in 1947, and since then, this song has influenced countless guitar legends from B. B. King to Jimi Hendrix. This particular version is based on the famous adaptation by The Allman Brothers Band, which features some sophisticated chord changes (especially in bars 7–10). Have fun with this one!

Cloudy Day Blues

Track 18

Lesson 5: Soloing in a Blues Style

One of the great things about the blues is that it makes full use of the expressive potential of the guitar. That means becoming as fluent as possible with the expressive techniques covered in the rock chapter, like bending, slides, hammer-ons, and pull-offs. The following blues solo licks also feature an extensive use of *vibrato*, a "warbling" effect produced by a series of quick, tiny bends. Combine these expressive techniques with a strong knowledge of the fretboard, and you have the makings of a killer blues solo. Where can you get some of that good note knowledge? Scales are a great place to start.

The three scale patterns below illustrate how to take a common pentatonic scale and turn it into two more useful scales: the *blues scale*, and the *composite blues scale*. It can't be overemphasized how much mileage you can get from these three related patterns. First, take a look at how these scale shapes are connected. Then, try out some of the classic blues licks that follow. Once you get some of these riffs under your fingers, try to play them over the blues tunes in this chapter. All of these riff examples are in the key of E Minor, but they can all be transposed to any key and they can be used over a dominant blues or a minor blues. Also, some (but not all) of the following blues riffs come directly from the three scale patterns below. See if you can figure out which ones correspond.

This familiar pentatonic scale pattern with the root on the 6th string provides an incredibly strong foundation for blues soloing.

Now, add the ♭5 (known as a *blue note*) to create the blues scale. Feel free to approach the blue note (indicated below with ◉) from above or below.

Finally, add the major 3rd (indicated below with ○) to your scale. This note sounds great when it is approached from below by way of a slide or hammer-on.

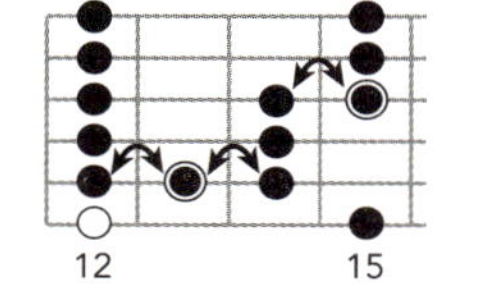

1) The pentatonic scale

2) The blues scale

3) The composite blues scale

Blues Licks

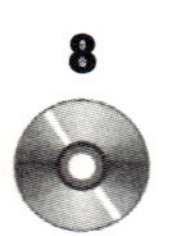

8

Track 19

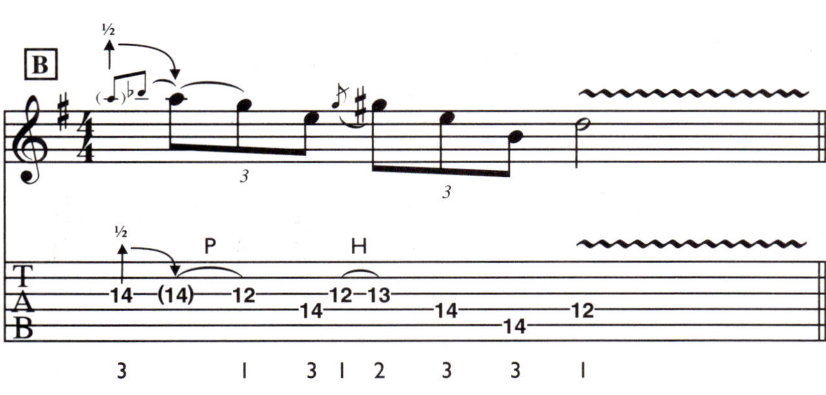

= Vibrato

= *Bend and release.* Bend up to the indicated pitch then bring the string back down to the original pitch.

= *Prebend and release.* Before sounding the string, bend it up to the indicated pitch. Pick the string, then release the bend to its original note.

C
Swing 8ths

D

E

F

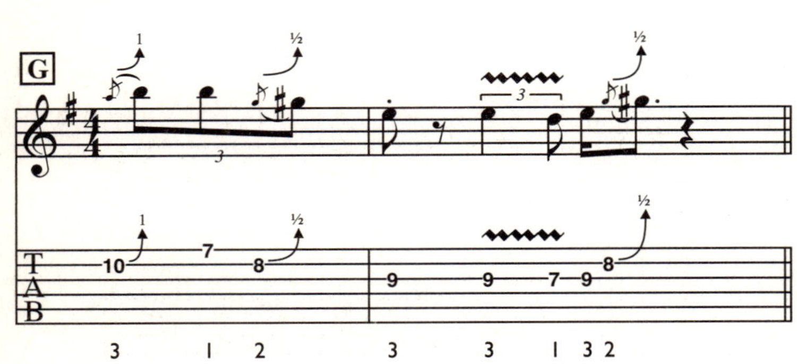
G

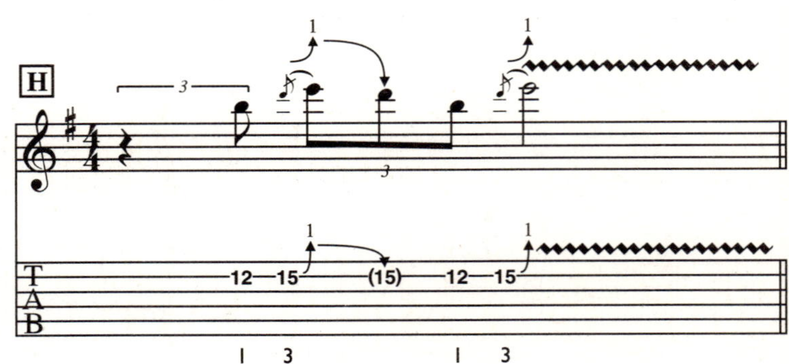
H

CHAPTER FOUR
ACOUSTIC GUITAR

+ +

Lesson 1: Slash Chords and the Bass/Strum

The acoustic steel-string guitar encompasses many traditional genres of music like folk, blues, country, and bluegrass, as well as numerous contemporary styles like rock and pop. In addition, there are some styles that have become unequivocally associated with the acoustic guitar, such as the singer-songwriter style.

Since the singer-songwriter style often consists of a single performer simultaneously singing and accompanying themselves on the guitar, certain techniques have been developed in order to maximize the scope of the instrument. In this respect, one of the most effective techniques for guitar accompaniment is the *bass/strum* style. In this style, the strumming pattern consists of doing just what the name implies: play a bass note and then strum the chord. Because of the rhythmic independence of the bass notes, special passing chords, known as *slash chords* (whose lowest note is not the root), are often employed to create smooth bass lines between the primary chords in the progression. In addition, slash chords can also be used to embellish the harmony of a song. The example below is in the style of "Another Lonely Day" by Ben Harper, and it features the bass/chord rhythm style and two different types of slash chords.

Afternoon Again

Track 20

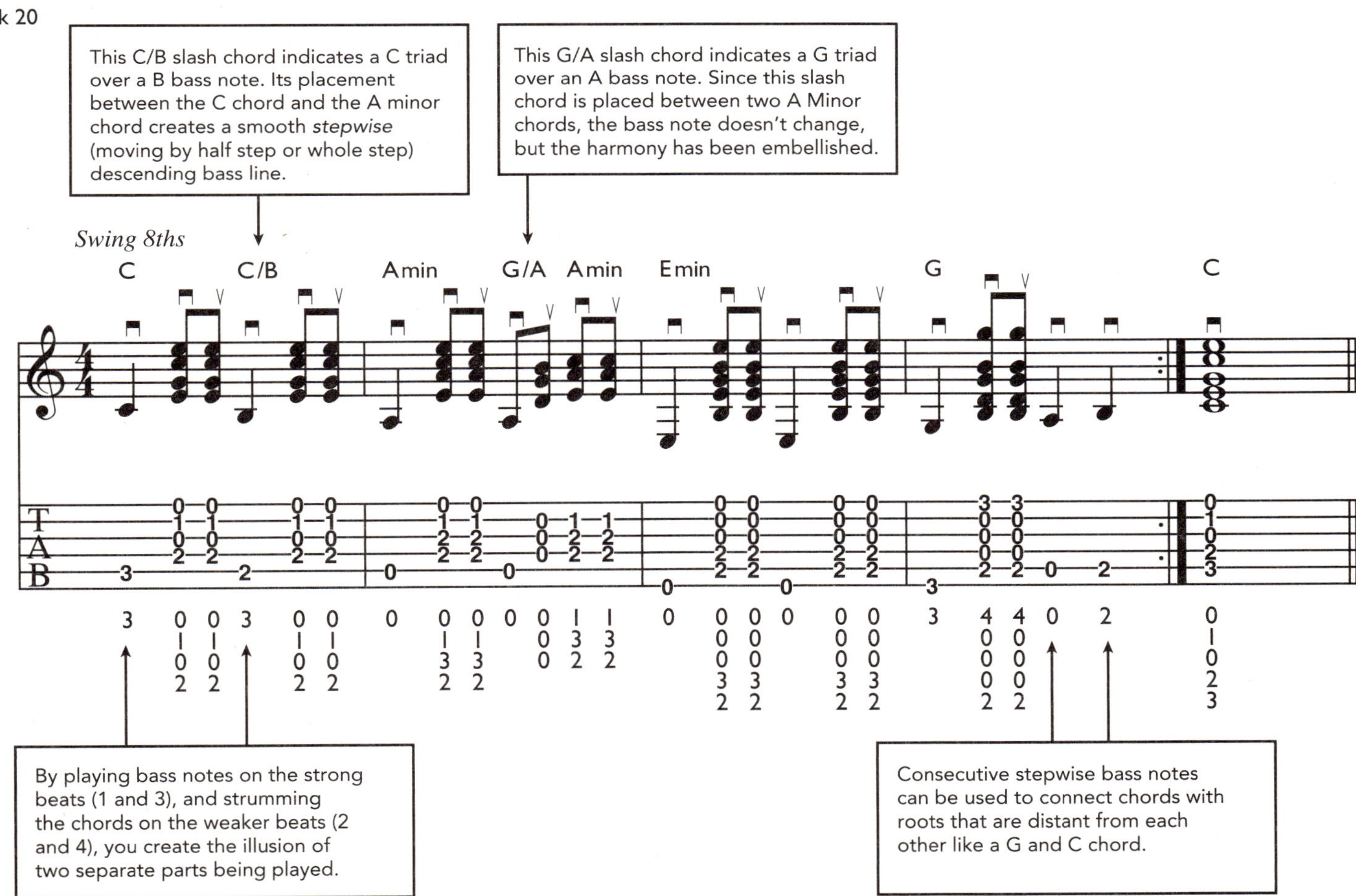

Here is a tune in the style of "Say Yes" by singer-songwriter Elliott Smith. Similar to the previous example, this song incorporates the bass/strum technique as well as slash chords. However, in this case, the song is built from movable chords rather than open chords, so you can use these voicings in any key by shifting them up and down the fretboard.

These slash chords function to create a long descending bass line over a static harmony. The F chord on top stays stationary, while the bass moves by step.

Absolutely

Track 21

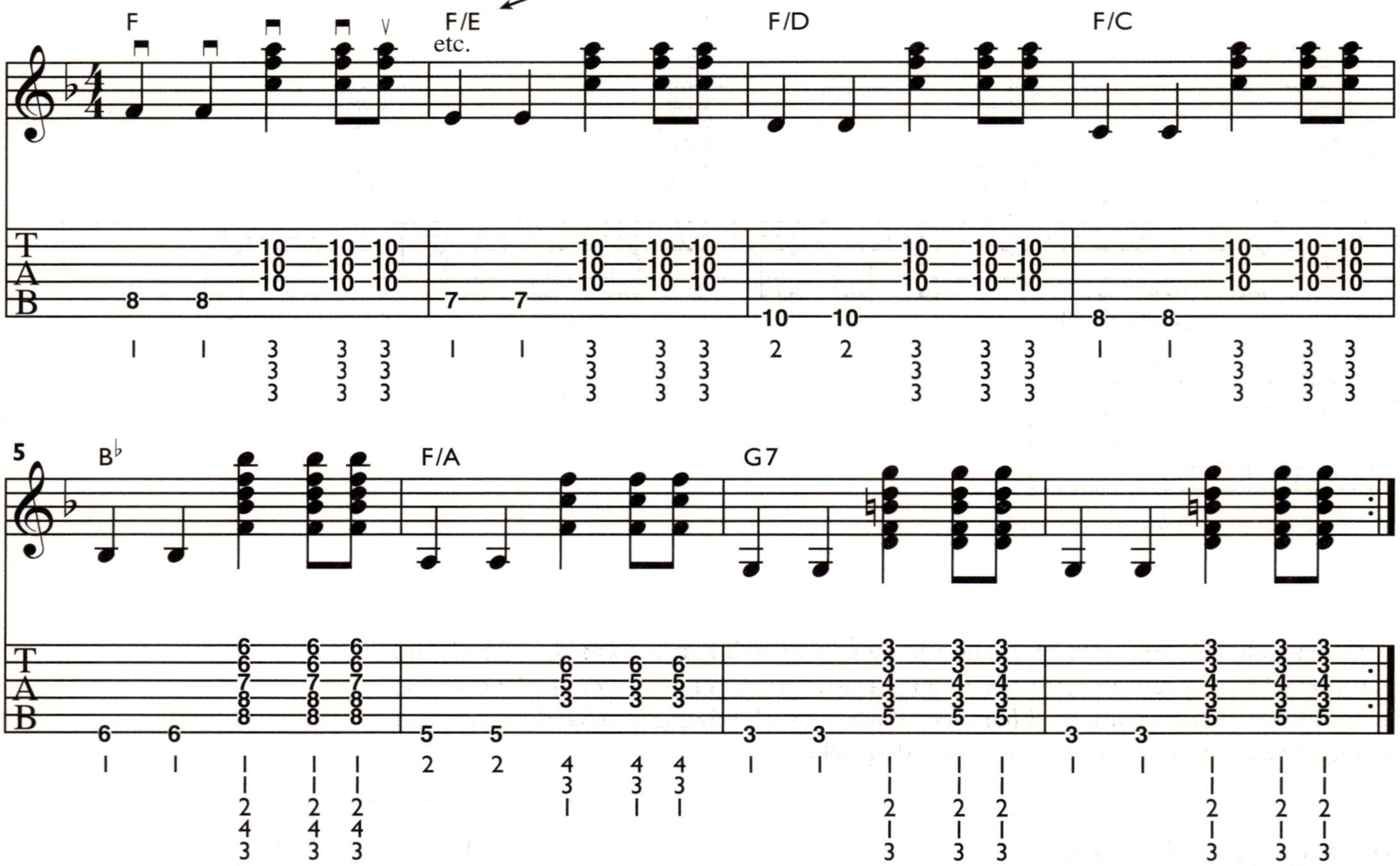

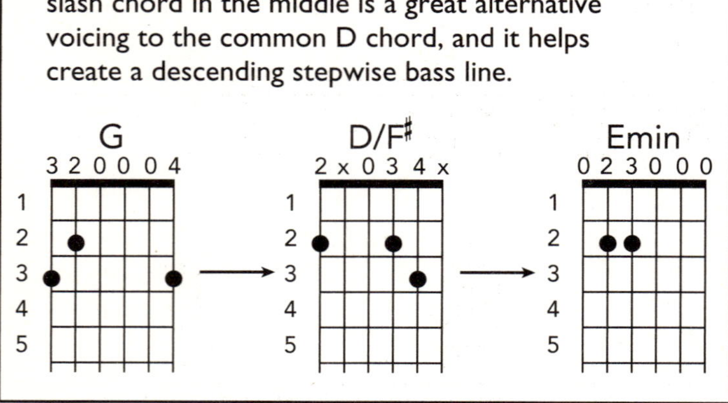

Check out the chord progression below. The slash chord in the middle is a great alternative voicing to the common D chord, and it helps create a descending stepwise bass line.

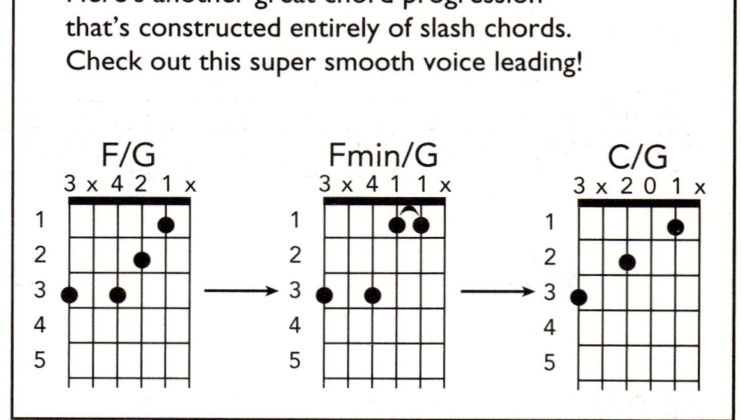

Here's another great chord progression that's constructed entirely of slash chords. Check out this super smooth voice leading!

Lesson 2: The Quintessential Strum

Let's take a look at a quintessential acoustic strumming pattern. Over the years, it's been used in countless songs from traditional folk music to modern acoustic rock. To illustrate this rhythm, take a look at the next example, which is in the style of the song "Half the World Away" by the band Oasis. Notice how the strumming pattern features two consecutive upstrums in the middle of each bar? These upstrums on the "&" of beats 2 and 3 create a strong sense of *syncopation*, which means accenting the offbeats rather than the beats.

Half a Strum to Play

Track 22

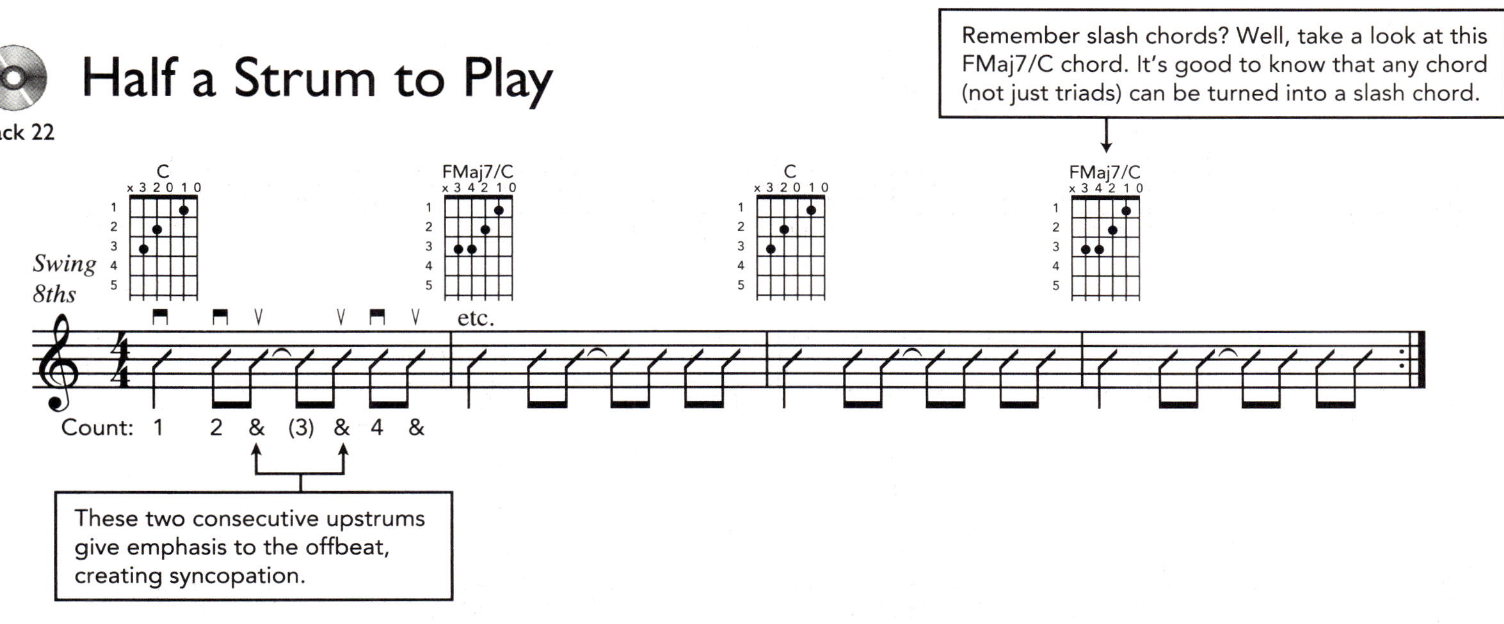

The next example is in the style of the classic tune "Simple Twist of Fate" by Bob Dylan, and guess what? It features the same strumming pattern as the previous example! However, the tempo, chord progression, and *harmonic rhythm* (see below) are quite different, and that's what keeps these two tunes from sounding alike.

A Twist of Lime

Track 23

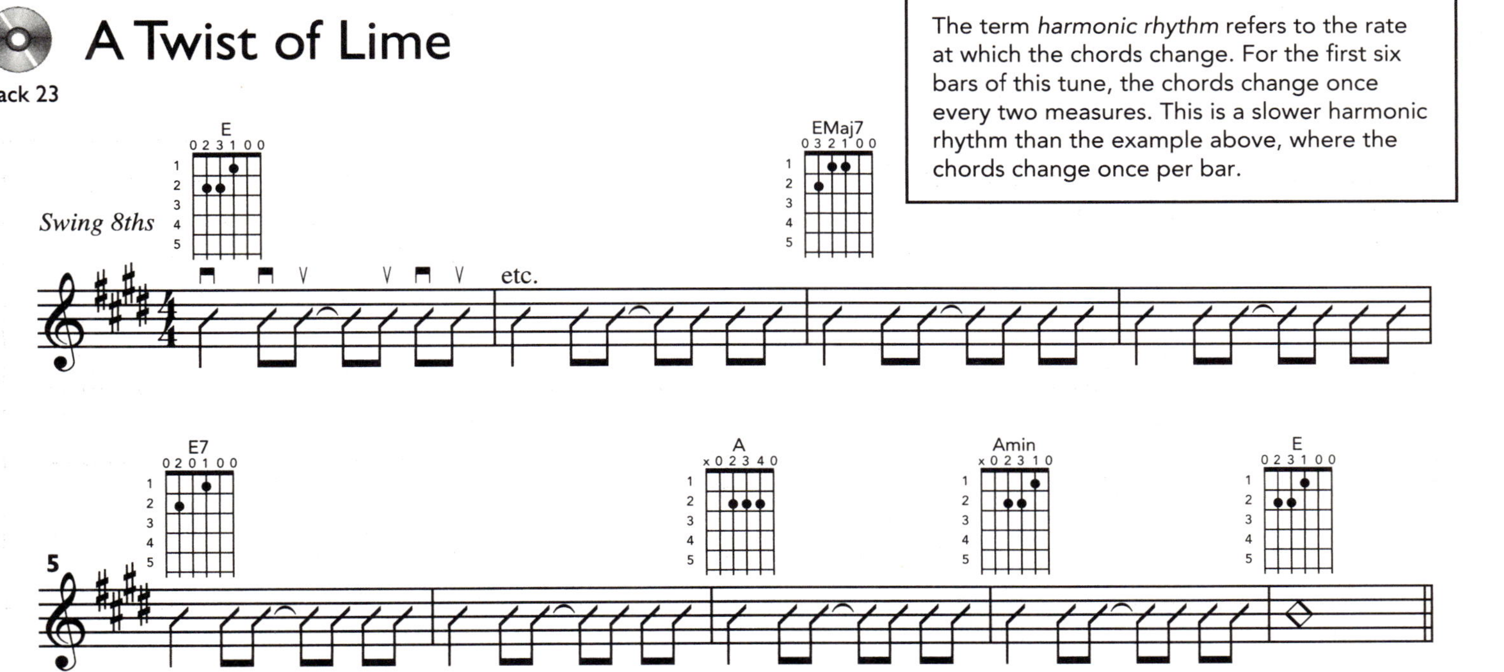

Lesson 3: The Muted Strum

The *muted strum* is a technique that's widely used by acoustic guitarists. In particular, artists like Jack Johnson have finely honed this type of playing to give their guitar accompaniment a percussive feel. There are two different, yet equally useful, ways to create this effect. One involves the strumming hand and the other involves the fretting hand. Let's take a look at both.

Muting with the Fretting Hand

Here's how to create a muted strum with the fretting hand:

Step 1) Build a 5th fret A Minor barre chord.

Step 2) Release the pressure of the fretting hand slightly so that you are no longer fretting the chord. However, make sure your left-hand fingers maintain contact with all six strings.

Step 3) Keep the fretting hand steady and give it a strum. You should hear a percussive slap.

Step 4) As an exercise, alternate between strumming a fretted barre chord and a muted strum (as shown below).

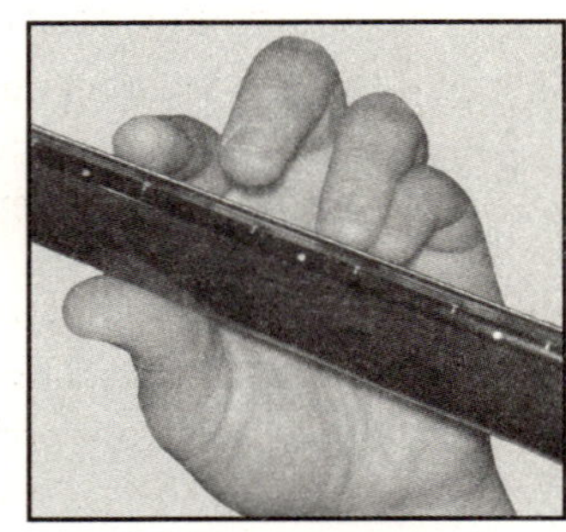

The fret-hand mute.

Fret-Hand Mute

Track 24

$\bigg\uparrow$ = Muted strum

Now try the same technique with an example in the style of "Sitting, Waiting, Wishing" by Jack Johnson. Even though the rhythm is more active than the previous example, try to accent the muted strums on beats two and four. This creates the feeling of a *backbeat*, which emulates the sound of a snare drum (normally the snare drum plays on beats 2 and 4 in rock and R&B styles).

Take a Seat

Track 25

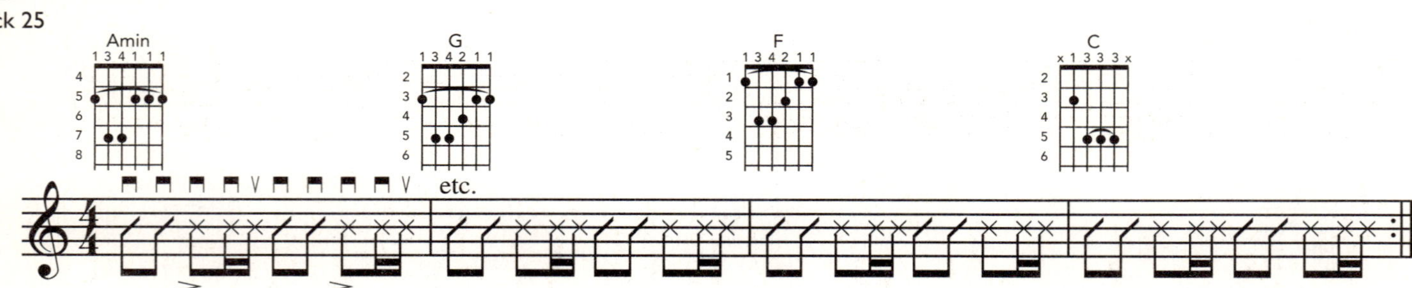

Muting with the Strumming Hand

Here's how to create a muted strum with the strumming hand:

Step 1) Form a 5th fret A Minor barre chord.

Step 2) In the strumming hand, place your palm over the strings as you would with a palm mute. However, make sure the palm is not placed near the bridge as it would be with a palm mute. Instead, place it anywhere near the sound hole.

Step 3) With the palm in place, deliver a sharp strum across all six strings. You should hear a percussive slap.

Step 4) Try alternating between strumming a fretted barre chord and a strumming hand mute similar to what you did with the "Fret-Hand Mute" on the previous page.

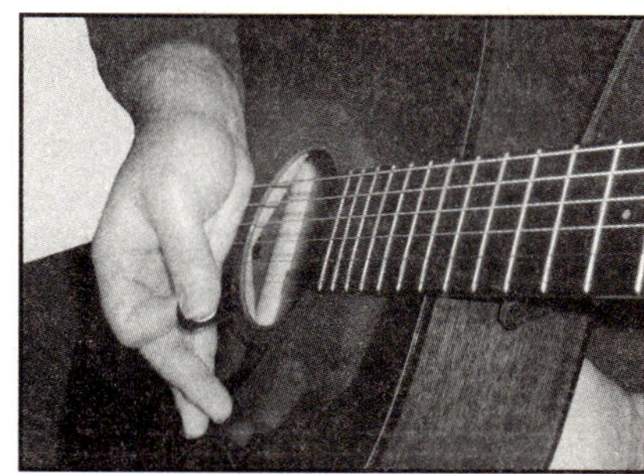

The strumming-hand mute.

With practice, this technique is just as accessible as muting with the fretting hand. In fact, when you are dealing with open chords, the strumming-hand mute technique is often preferred. It's also worth mentioning that many people actually use both techniques at the same time. When the fret hand as well as the strumming hand are generating the muted strum, a solid "chuck" is guaranteed. For practice, try the next two examples with a strumming-hand mute. Both examples are written in the style of Jack Johnson.

Moments Like Those

Track 26

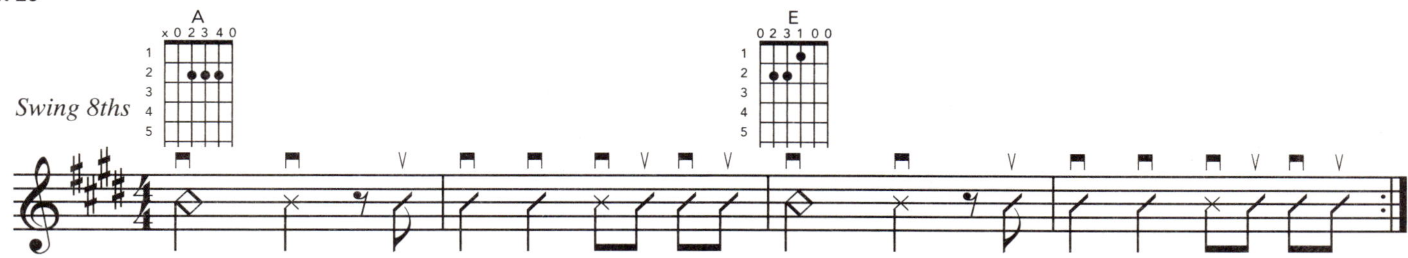

Flap

Track 27

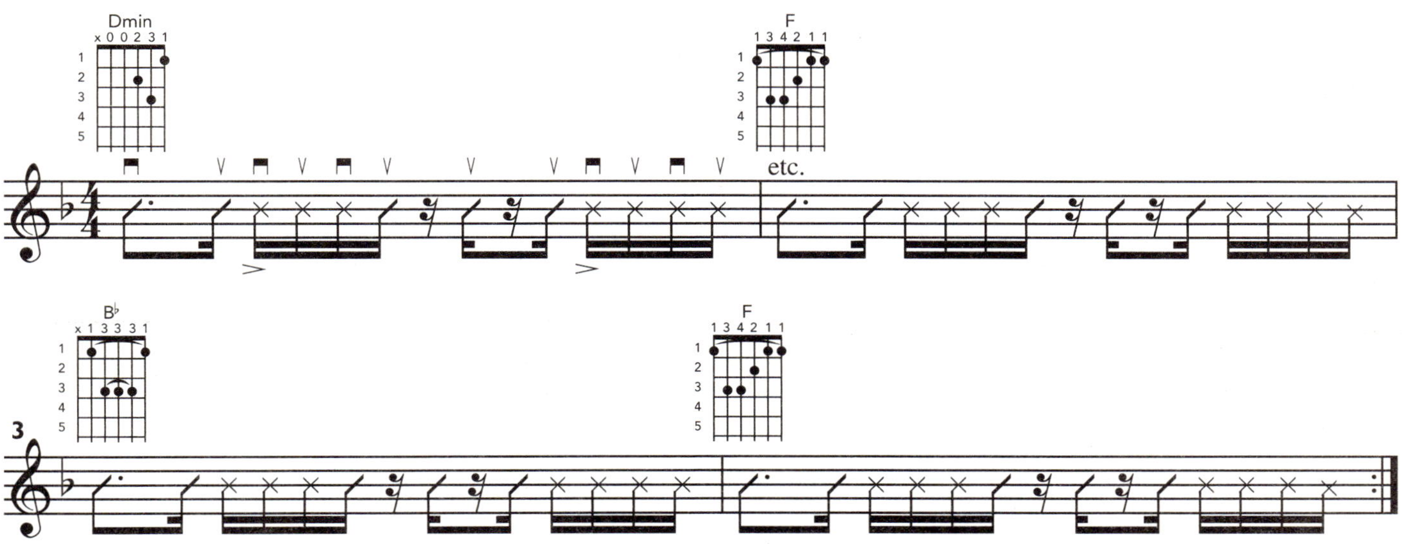

Lesson 4: Tricky Strumming Simplified

As a guitarist working with acoustic styles, strumming is a skill that is fundamentally important to develop. Since some of the strumming patterns you encounter will be simple, and some will be quite complex, it's good to know some tricks to simplify the more complicated patterns into something that's easy to count.

How is this achieved? The answer is creative counting. Luckily, if you can count to four then you are halfway there. And if you can verbalize "1–2–3–4," then it might not be that much of a stretch to verbalize "1–&, 2–&, 3–&, 4–&." This is a crucial skill to develop because it opens you up to the world of subdivision. On the surface, this skill allows you to accurately count eighth notes. But as you will soon see, it allows you to do a whole lot more as well.

A common method for sixteenth-note counting is to verbalize "1–e–&–a, 2–e–&–a, 3–e–&–a, 4–e–&–a." Suddenly the situation has become quite complicated because there are so many syllables to keep track of. While this method of counting does indeed work, you may find that this is a mouthful to pull off. So, here is a trick: In order to simplify the counting of sixteenth notes, visualize them as eighth notes. Something that will help a great deal with this method is called the *imaginary barline*. Take a look at the next example to see how this works. The rhythm and the chords are in the style of the modern acoustic hit "Crash into Me" by Dave Matthews.

This effectively cuts the tempo and the counting in half, so the quarter notes become half notes, the eighth notes become quarter notes and best of all, the sixteenth notes become eighth notes. Now it's much easier to count. Once you slowly count it through and get a feel for how the rhythm sounds, speed it back up, put it back into the progression, and you are ready to strum at full speed.

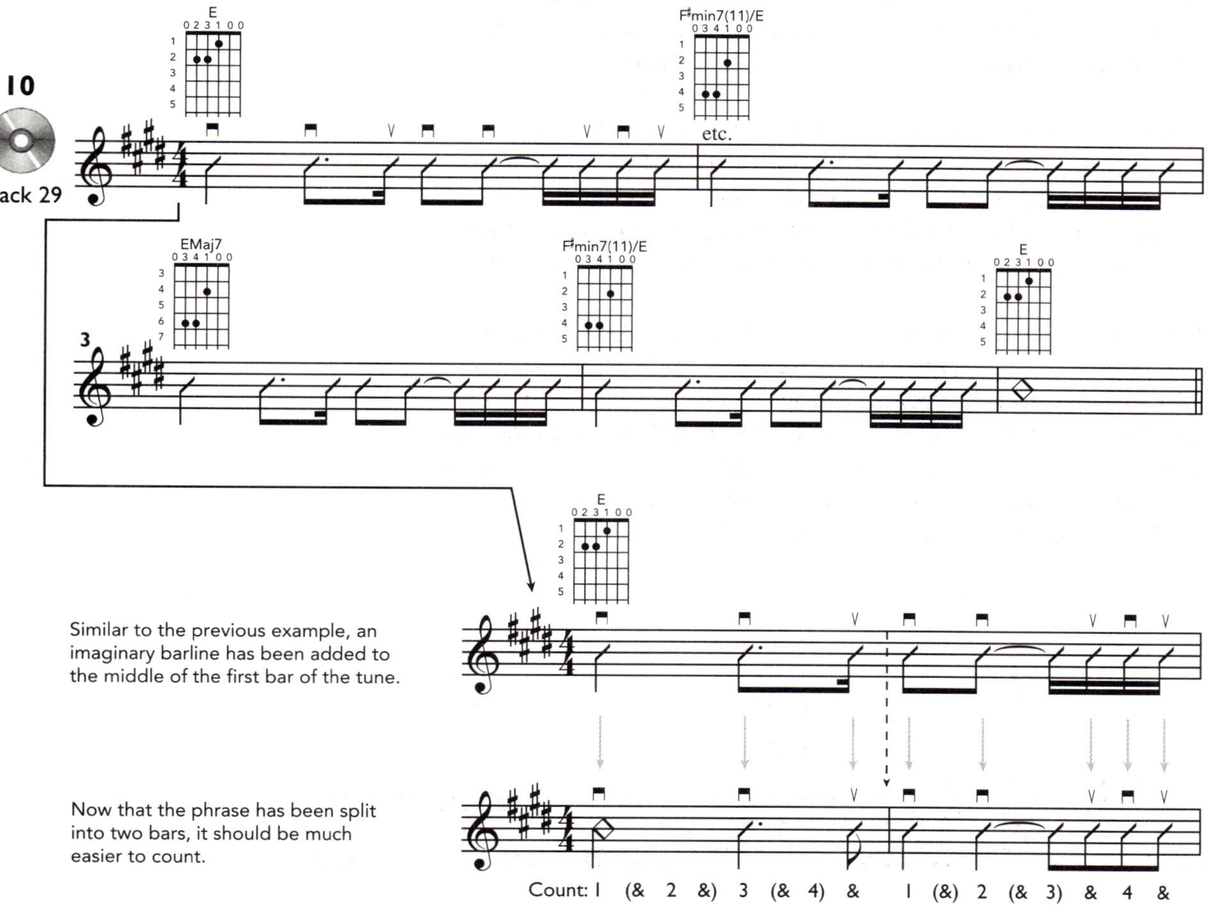

Here's another chance to see this rhythm-counting trick at work. The example below is in the style of "Sweet Melissa" by The Allman Brothers Band.

Now try to convert the next two song fragments on your own. The first one is based on "Collide" by Howie Day, and the second is based on "Black Horse and the Cherry Tree" by KT Tunstall. Good luck, and watch out for the mutes in these two examples.

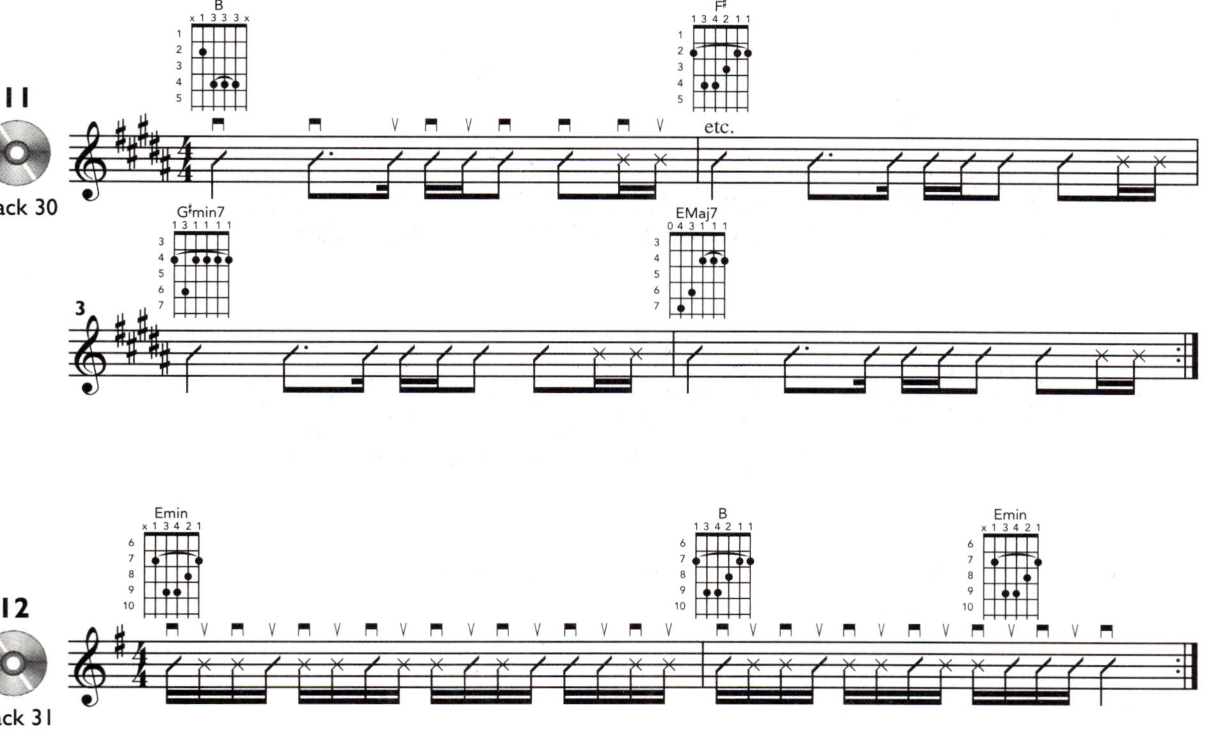

Lesson 5: Acoustic Soloing

The following licks feature essential acoustic soloing techniques such as sliding and double stops. They also feature another device common to acoustic soloing: combining open strings with fretted notes. Feel free to use these riffs over any song in the key of G Major.

D
G
Let ring
T A B

E
G
P P P
P P P
P P
P P
T A B

F
G
T A B

G
G
½
SL
SL P
½
T A B

CHAPTER FIVE
FINGERSTYLE GUITAR

++

Lesson 1: Pick Your Variation

Fingerstyle is a technique that employs various combinations of the right-hand thumb and fingers to pluck the strings. Depending on personal preference, fingerstyle players use different combinations of thumbpicks, fingerpicks, fingernails, or bare fingertips to pick the strings.

Regardless of whether you go with fingerpicks, fingernails, or bare skin, this is the basic home position for the picking hand: *p* (the thumb) plucks the 4th, 5th, or 6th strings, *i* (index) plucks the 3rd string, *m* (middle) plucks the 2nd string, and *a* (ring finger) plucks the 1st string. But as you will soon see, there are many other positions that are used. The following exercises are all played over an open E chord, but feel free to substitute your own chords for variety.

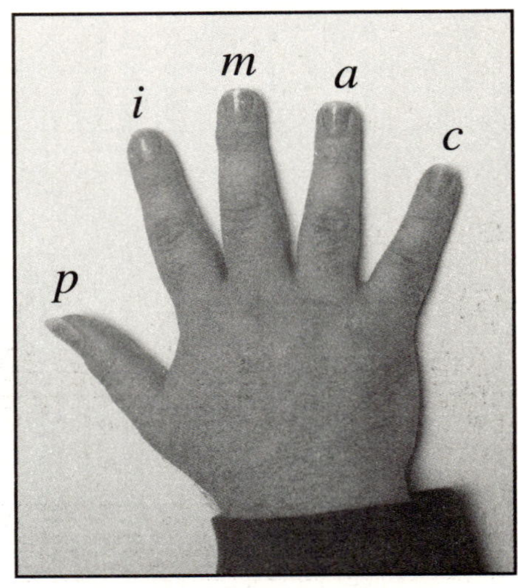

The right-hand fingers.

p Takes the Bottom Three

14 — Track 33

i, m, a Take the Top

p, i, m, a All the Way

The Pinch

The Pinch Plus One

The Cluster

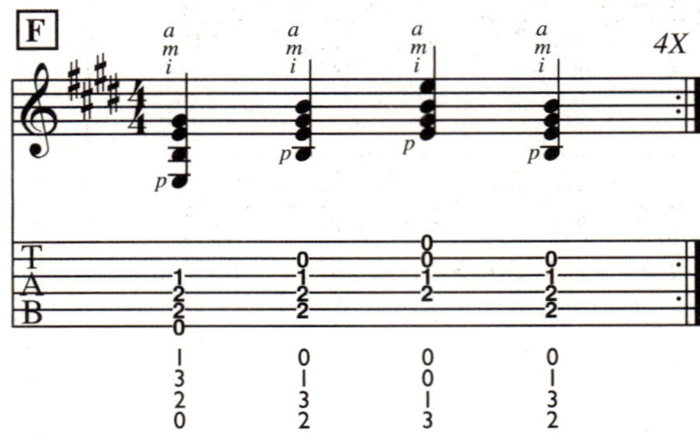

As you play through these examples, make sure your thumb strums downward, while your index, middle, and ring fingers pluck upwards, folding into the palm of the hand. Also, try to keep the thumb pointing out toward the neck as the illustration to the right shows. This helps to avoid any potential traffic jams between the thumb and the fingers.

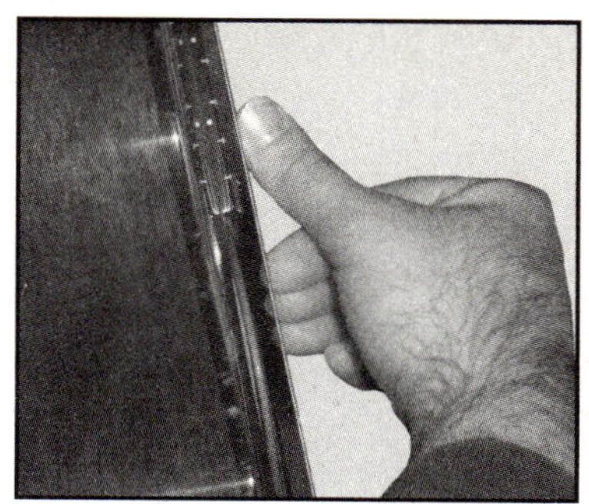

The right-hand thumb.

Displace the Pinch

Three in a Row

Four to Go

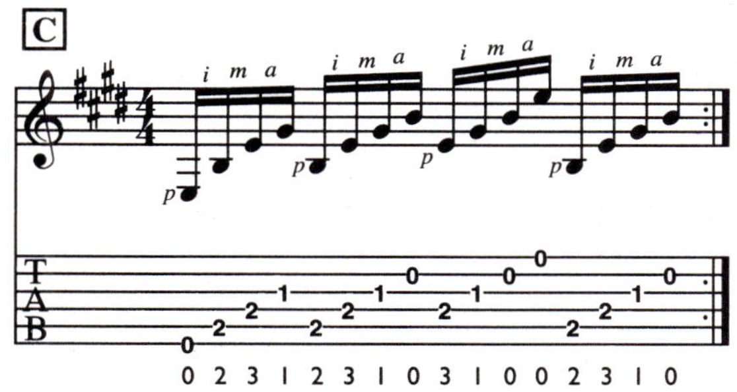

Walk the Bass

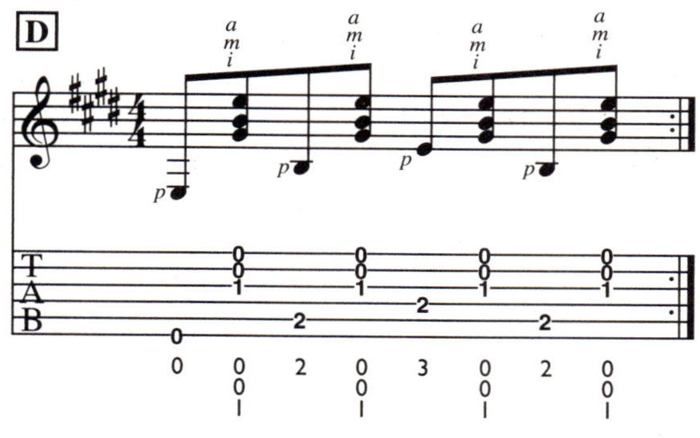

Split Up the Chords

Contrary Motion

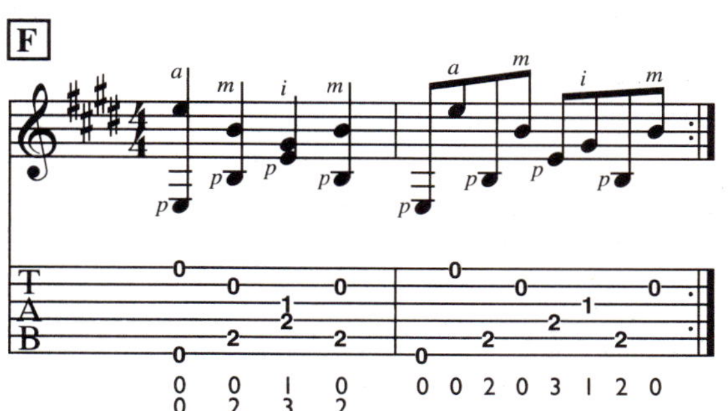

This page follows the development of two fingerpicking patterns, one in the left column and one in the right column. They both start simple at the top, but they get challenging as new elements are added.

Start with the Pinch

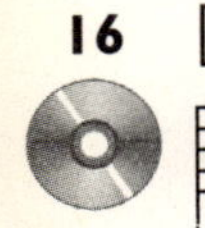

Add the *i*

Add the *a*

Alternate the *a*

Alternate the *p*

Displace the Pinch

Displace *p, i,* and *m*

Add *a* and Displace

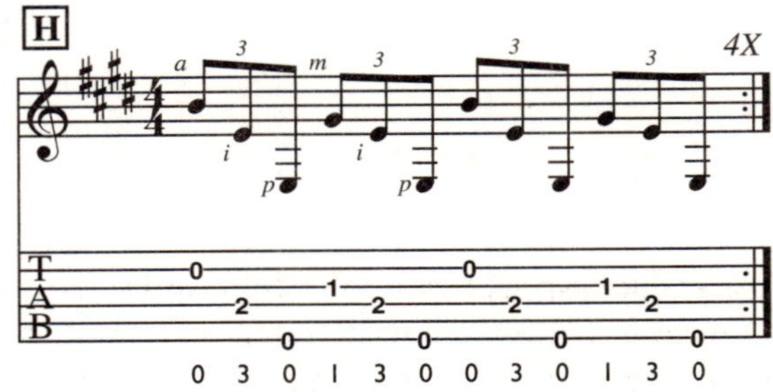

Displace and Alternate *a*

Displace and Alternate *p*

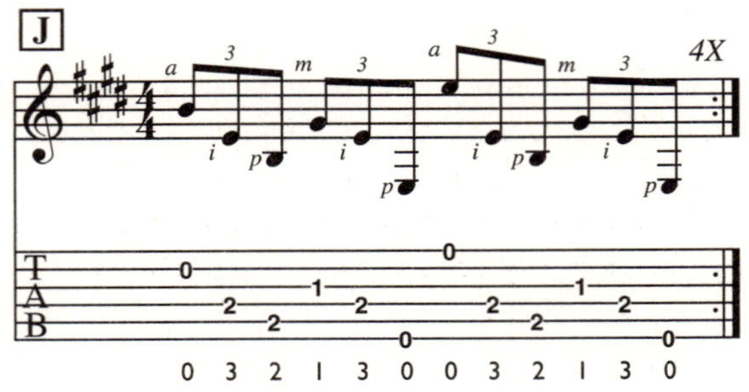

Lesson 2: Fingerpicking Potential

Now that you've worked with a variety of fingerpicking patterns, let's look at a tune that is completely pattern-based. It's called "Passenger Pigeon" and it's in the style of the fingerstyle classic "Blackbird" by Paul McCartney of the Beatles. And, you are in luck, because there are only two fingerpicking patterns in the whole piece.

Pattern 1

The first pattern is based on the pinch, which is placed on beats 1, 2, 3, and 4, with the index (*i*) added on the offbeats. Take a look at this pattern over an open G chord:

Pattern 2

To the right is the second fingerpicking pattern. The thumb (*p*) plucks on beats 1, 2, 3, and 4, while the middle (*m*) and index (*i*) create a syncopated pattern on top.

The first half of this etude also features a G Major scale that has been harmonized across the fretboard (the harmony is a diatonic 3rd plus an octave, otherwise known as a 10th). It's nice to realize that if you visualize this scale pattern in the right way, it can be simplified to only two shapes: a diagonal shape with a two-fret span and a diagonal shape with a three-fret span. Take a look at how these patterns line up:

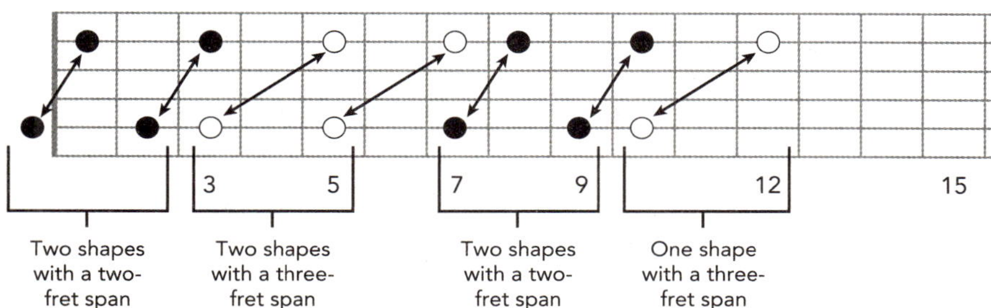

Try playing these patterns up and down the neck with your 1st finger on the 5th string and your 4th finger on the 2nd string. The solid black dots above indicate the diagonal shapes with a two-fret span, and the hollow dots indicate the diagonal shapes with a three-fret span. Be on the lookout for this fretboard pattern (as well as the two fingerpicking patterns above) as you play through "Passenger Pigeon" on the next page.

Passenger Pigeon

Track 37

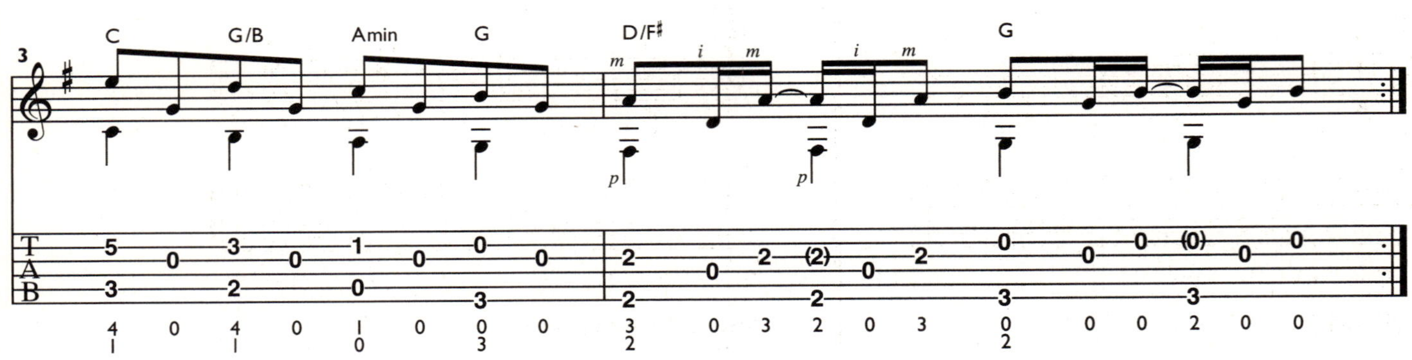

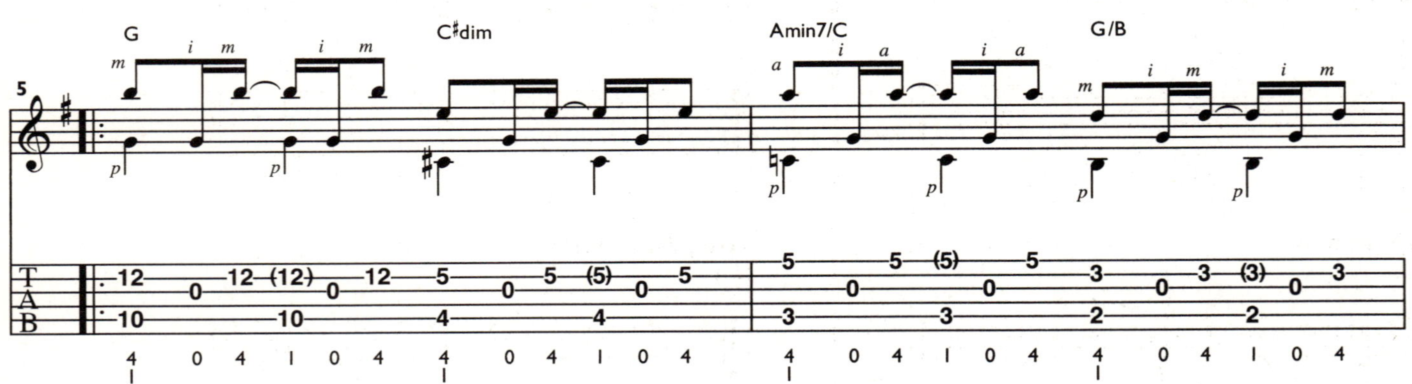

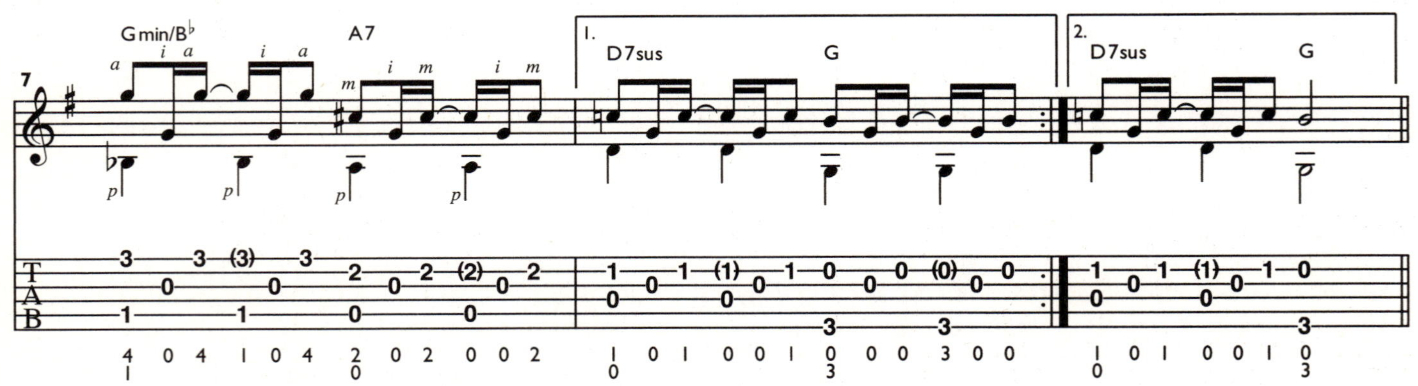

Lesson 3: Travis Picking

Travis picking is one of the most common (and downright fun) techniques available to fingerstyle guitarists. It's a style named after the great country/western fingerpicker Merle Travis, who developed a sophisticated alternate bass technique that influenced an entire generation of guitar players (Chet Atkins in particular). The Travis picking style has evolved into a technique that commonly includes the *p*, *i*, and *m* fingers (however, it's good to know Merle Travis only used his thumb and index finger).

In the examples below, the column to the left illustrates how to construct a basic Travis picking pattern over a C chord. The column to the right shows how to develop the basic pattern into more complicated sequences. Once you get comfortable with the following examples, try the "Travis Rag" on the next page.

Start with *p* and *m*

18

Track 38

A

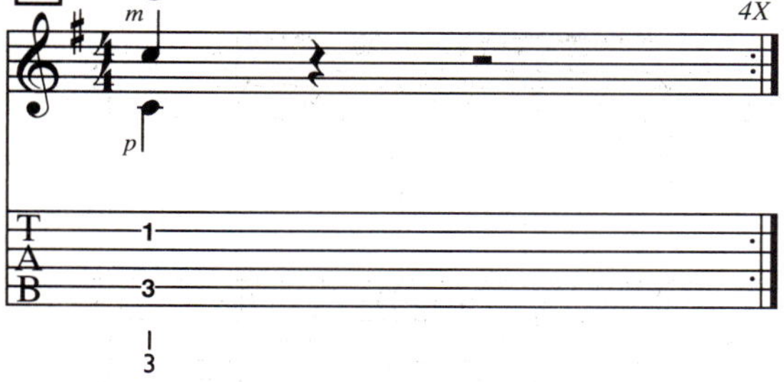

Add *p* and *i*

B

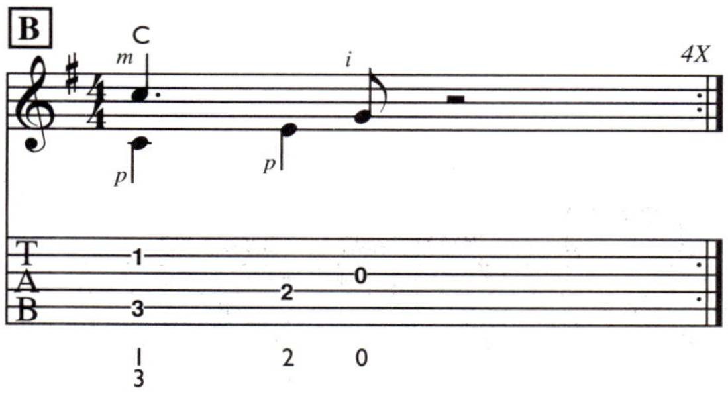

Add *p* and *m*

C

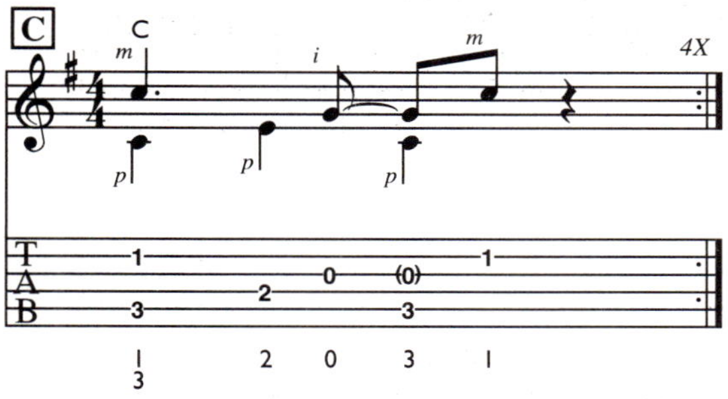

Add *p*

D

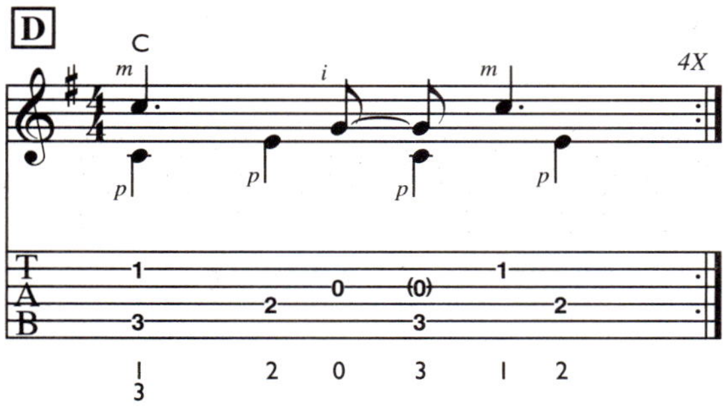

Add *i* on the "&" of Beat Four

E

Now, Alternate *m*

F

Now, Alternate *p*

G

Add Palm Mute and Swing

H

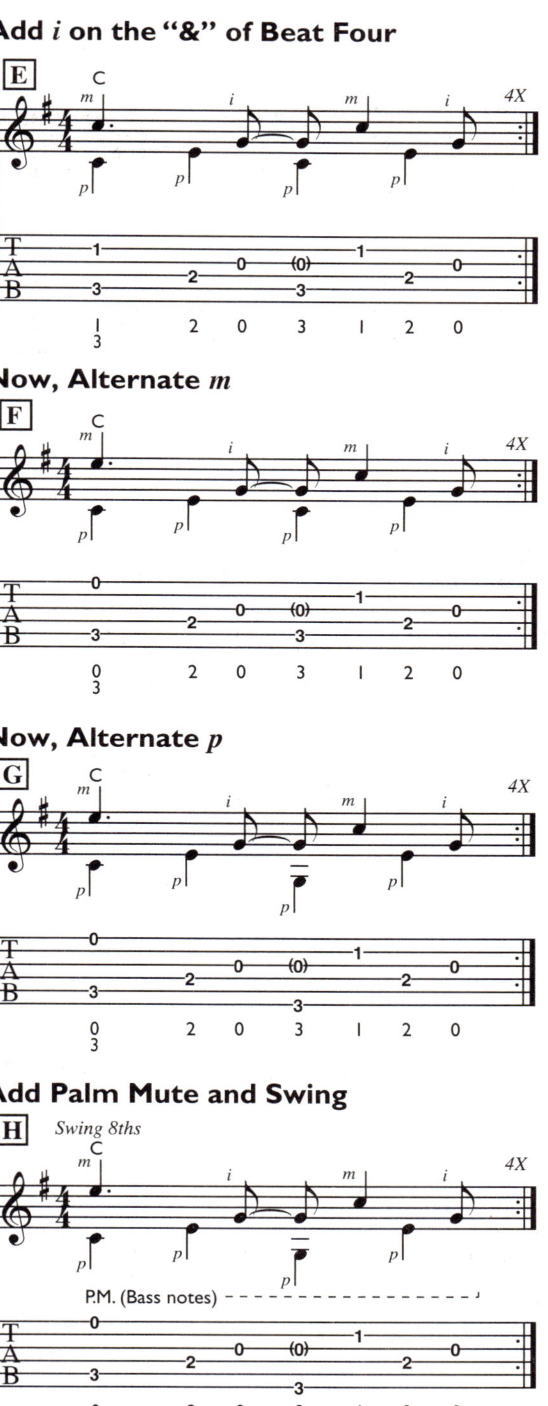

The "Travis Rag" is a tune written in the style of Merle Travis. It features a sophisticated Travis picking pattern plus a few bonus musical tricks that are common to this style. In particular, watch out for a fancy turnaround in bars 7 and 8. Then, get ready for a triplet roll in bar 15, finishing up with a C6 chord at the very end. Once you get the pattern down, try adding a palm mute to the bass notes.

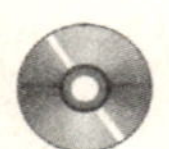

Travis Rag

Track 39

    The Guitar Style Resource

Lesson 4: Melodic Fingerpicking

"Fingerpicking Paradise" is a tune written in the style of "Tears in Heaven" by Eric Clapton. It's a prime example of a style of voice leading where the top note of each chord creates a smooth step-wise melody. Here are some distinct features of this arrangement:

1) The tune includes numerous slash chords, which help create smooth, melodic voice leading.

2) The *a* finger plays the melody for most of the piece.

3) The pinky (designated by the letter *c*) takes the melody for the last three bars of the piece.

4) The last chord is an Asus2 chord. Sus2 chords are a common substitute for major (and even minor) chords. They create a very open, tranquil, and somewhat ambiguous sound.

Fingerpicking Paradise

Track 40

CHAPTER SIX
CLASSICAL GUITAR

+ +

Lesson 1: Posture and Positioning

Six-string classical guitars were first built in Spain around 1790. However, it's only been in the last 100 years that modern classical guitar construction has become relatively standardized—based on the revolutionary designs of the Spanish luthier Antonio de Torres Jurado. The modern classical guitar features distinct characteristics, including nylon strings (the three bass strings are generally wound with silver plated copper, but still feature a threaded nylon core), tuning machines that are perpendicular to the neck, and a wide, flat fretboard.

Over the centuries, a rich heritage of great players, arrangers, and composers have established standard techniques and repertoire for the classical guitar. But, before we delve into aspects of playing and performance, let's take a look at classical guitar posture. The guitar is held in place by: 1) the lower portion of the chest, 2) the upper portion of the left thigh, 3) the inner portion of the right thigh, and 4) the underside of the right forearm.

Classical guitar posture, front view. The footstool raises the neck to the optimum angle for comfortable playing.

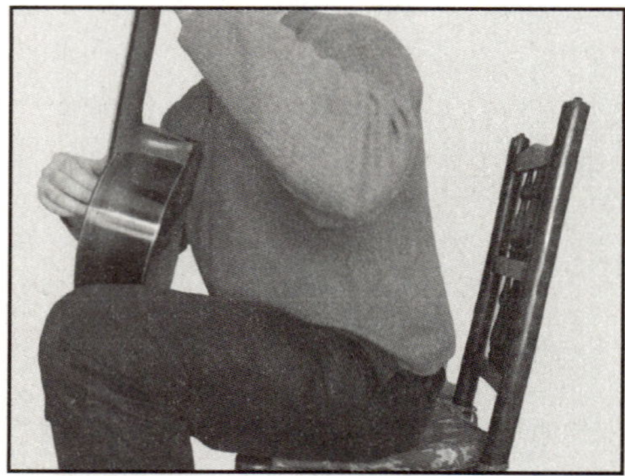

Classical guitar posture, side view. Make sure there is space between the back of the guitar and the stomach for best tone and sound projection.

This device and others like it provide an alternative to the footstool. It allows the guitarist to keep both feet flat, thereby straightening out the spine.

The placement of the right and left hands in relation to the guitar is just as important as posture. All together, the goal is to keep the hands, limbs, body, and mind in a state free from tension. The images below illustrate proper hand and wrist placement for the classical guitar, although the same principles can be applied to other styles as well.

Left-Hand Positioning

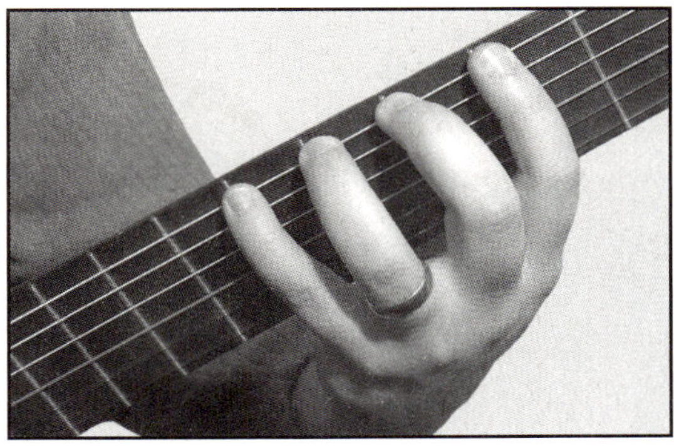

Place the fingers directly behind the frets, and line up the thumb with the second finger.

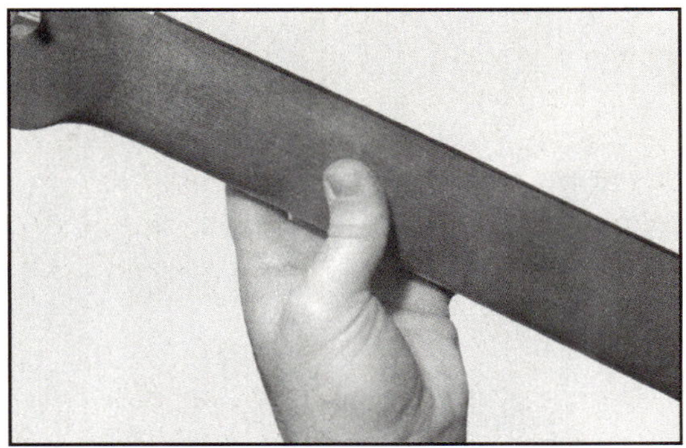

Keep the wrist straight, placing the thumb near the middle of the back of the neck.

Right-Hand Positioning

Notice how the thumb points to the neck, staying out of the way of the fingers. Also, the wrist is straight.

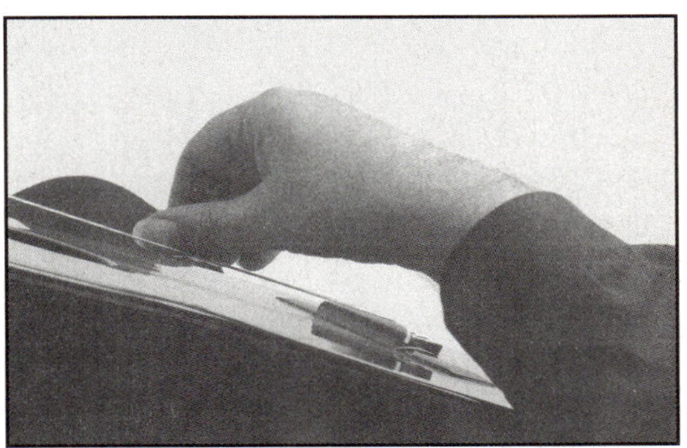

Here is another view of the thumb from above.

Shaping the Fingernails

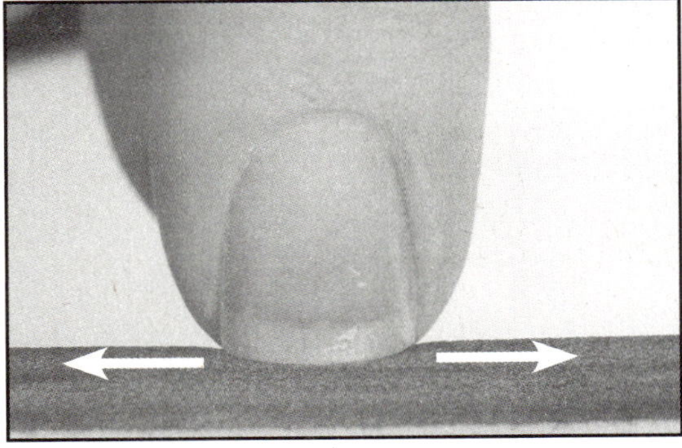

File the fingernails so that a "ramp" is created for the strings.

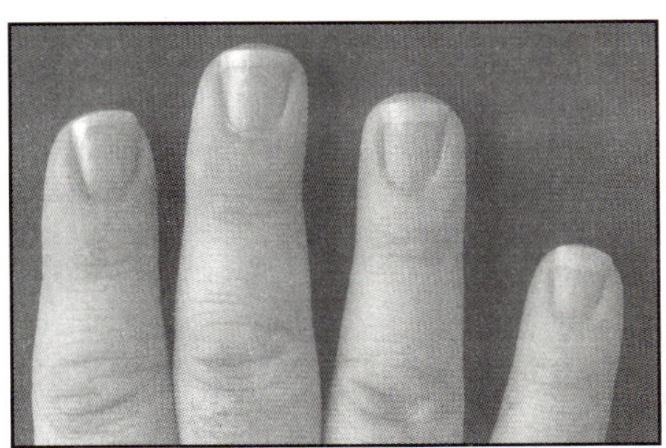

The nails should extend as far as the fingertips. The thumbnail can be a bit longer.

Lesson 2: Classical Fingerpicking

In the fingerstyle chapter, it was mentioned that the pick-hand thumb, index, middle, ring, and pinky are assigned letters for identification. These letters correspond to the Spanish terms listed to the right.

In the classical guitar style, there are two fundamental techniques for picking the strings: the *free stroke* (also known as *tirando*) and the *rest stroke* (also known as *apoyando*).

> Thumb = *p* (for *pulgar*)
> Index = *i* (for *indice*)
> Middle = *m* (for *medio*)
> Ring = *a* (for *annular*)
> Pinky = *c* (for *chico*)

Free Stroke

A free stroke is accomplished by plucking the string in such a way that the follow-through of the picking finger curls in toward the heel of the hand, missing the adjacent string. (See photos below.)

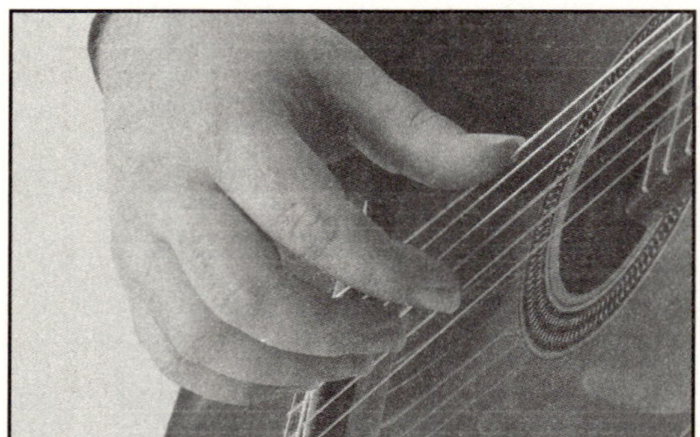

Preparing for a free stroke.

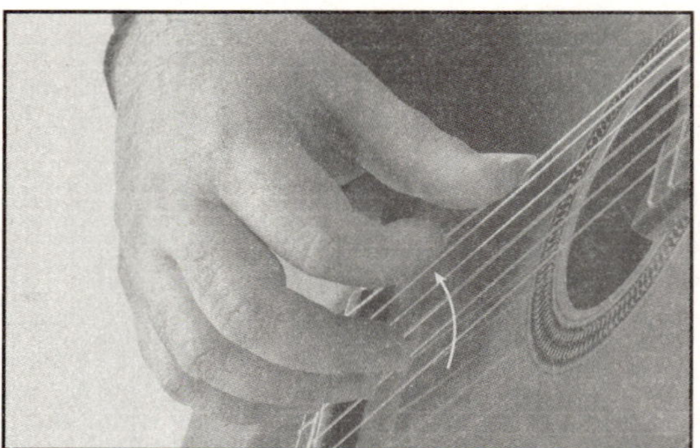

Free stroke follow-through.

Rest Stroke

A rest stroke is accomplished by plucking the string in such a way that the follow-through of the picking finger comes to rest on the adjacent string. (See photos below.)

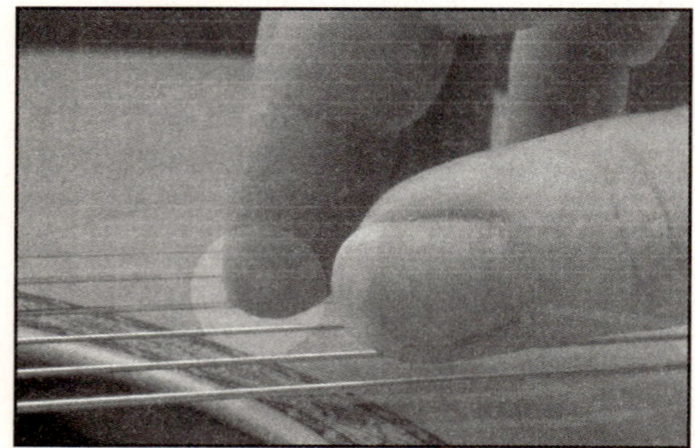

Preparing for a rest stroke.

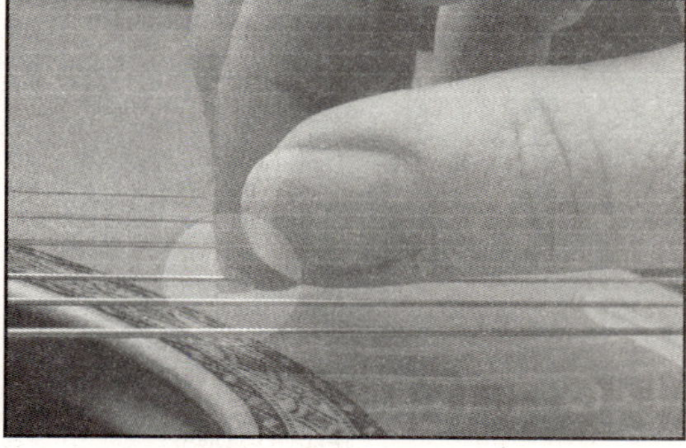

Rest stroke follow-through.

Controlling Your Tone

The tone of your guitar is greatly affected by where you pluck the strings. To get a sharp, bright tone, pluck near the bridge; this technique is indicated by the term *sul ponticello*. To get a deep, warm tone, pluck over the soundhole or closer to the neck; this technique is indicated by the term *sul tasto*.

Warm-Up Exercise

It's a great idea to warm up before playing. To get your right hand going, take a C Major scale and play it using the following right-hand finger combinations: 1) *i–m–i–m*, etc., 2) *m–a–m–a*, etc., 3) *i–a–i–a*, etc. Play through these right-hand fingerings first using free strokes, then rest strokes.

Lesson 3: The Renaissance and Baroque Periods

The three examples that follow were composed before the modern classical guitar was invented. "Greensleeves" is a famous theme from the Renaissance period (ca. 1400–1600) that would have originally been played on a lute. The $\frac{6}{8}$ time signature indicates six eighth notes per measure. It is counted as two groups of three: "**1**–&–ah, **2**–&–ah."

Greensleeves

Track 41

The best-known composer from the Baroque period (ca. 1685–1750) is Johann Sebastian Bach. Here are the first eight bars (with a full D chord at the end for a sense of finality) of the prelude from Bach's "Cello Suite No. 1." It features a D bass note that is repeated throughout, while the harmony changes above it (this is called a *pedal tone*). The pedal tone is facilitated by *drop D tuning*, in which the 6th string is tuned down a whole step from E to D.

Cello Suite No. 1 (Prelude)

Track 42

Practicing music on the classical guitar can sometimes feel like putting together a jigsaw puzzle because there is often more than one melody going on at time. So, as you play through Bach's "Minuet in G," try to pay special attention to the fingerings. Smooth fingerings can make complicated music much easier to play.

Minuet in G

Track 43

Lesson 4: The Classical Period

Here are some musical examples that were composed for the guitar in the early 19th century during the Classical period (ca. 1750–1820). The first example is the first eight bars of a piece written by Mauro Giuliani. Get ready, because it's a real workout for the thumb.

Etude in A Minor

Track 44

The next example was composed by the Spanish guitarist Fernando Sor. This one's a workout for the *i* and *m* fingers.

Allegro in G

Track 45

Italian composer/guitarist Ferdinando Carulli wrote the next example entitled "Prelude in C."
In the early 19th century, Carulli was famous not only for his guitar compositions, but also for
authoring the first complete classical guitar method, which is still used today.

Prelude in C

Track 46

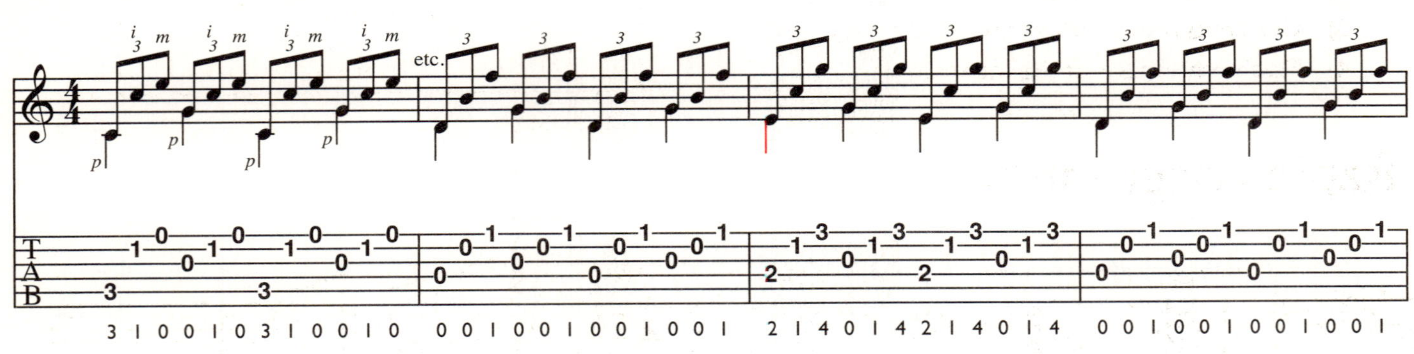

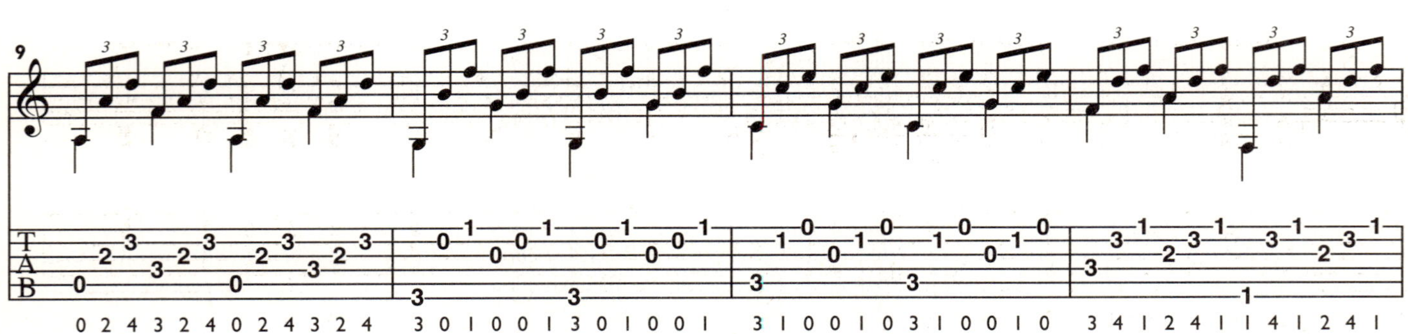

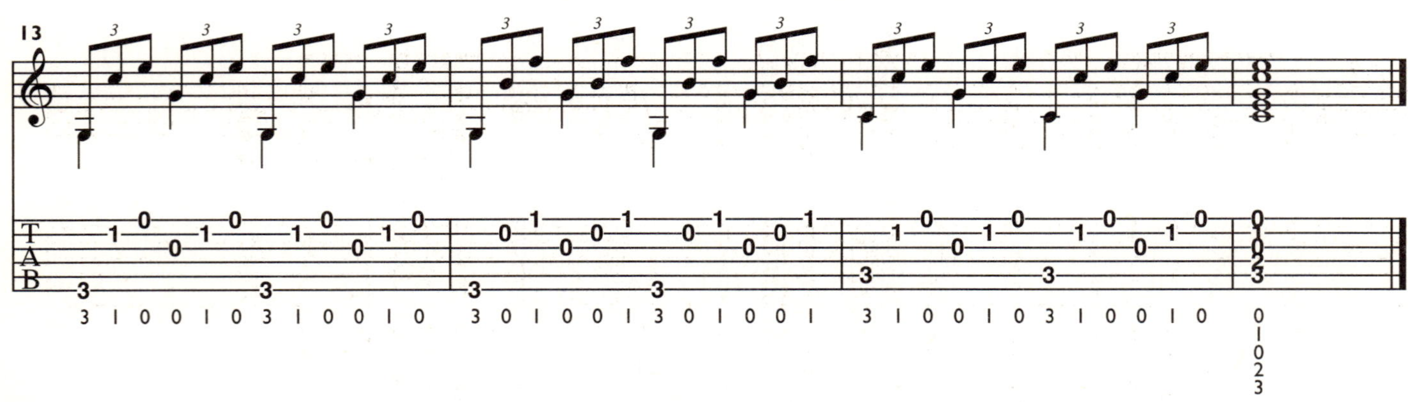

The Guitar Style Resource

Lesson 5: Flamenco Guitar

Flamenco is a Spanish art form with a rich tradition in song (known as *cante*), dance (called *baile*), and guitar (called *toque*). One of the most effective ways to get a feel for flamenco is through a strumming technique called *rasgueado*. Here's how to execute a common rasgueado pattern:

1) Strum with a flick of the pinky *(c)*
2) Continue with a flick of the ring finger *(a)*
3) Continue with a flick of the middle finger *(m)*
4) Finish with a flick of the index finger *(i)*

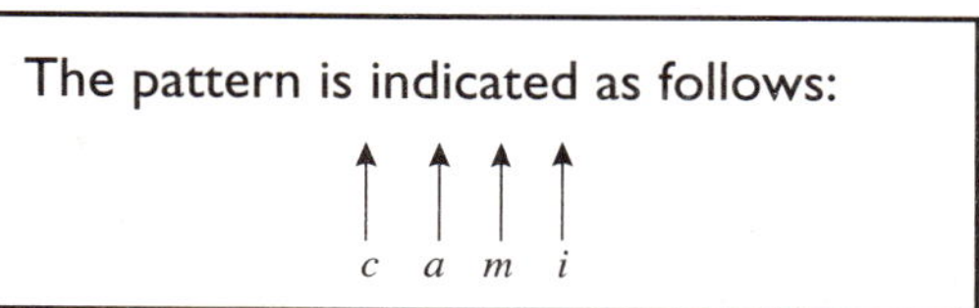

Rapid Rasgueados

Track 47

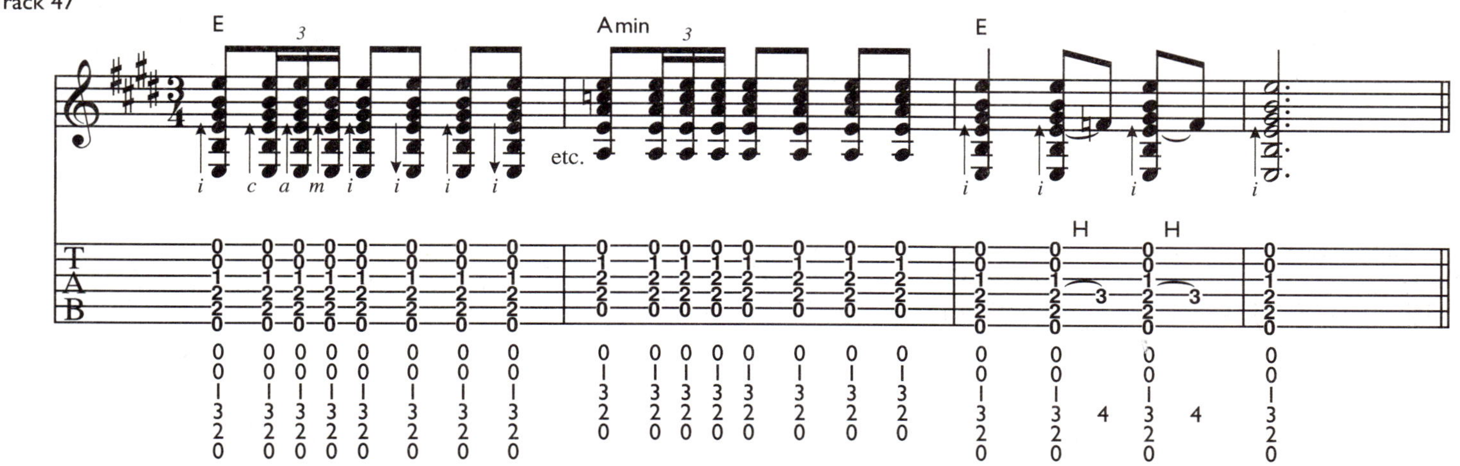

Flamenco Fingers Flying

Track 48

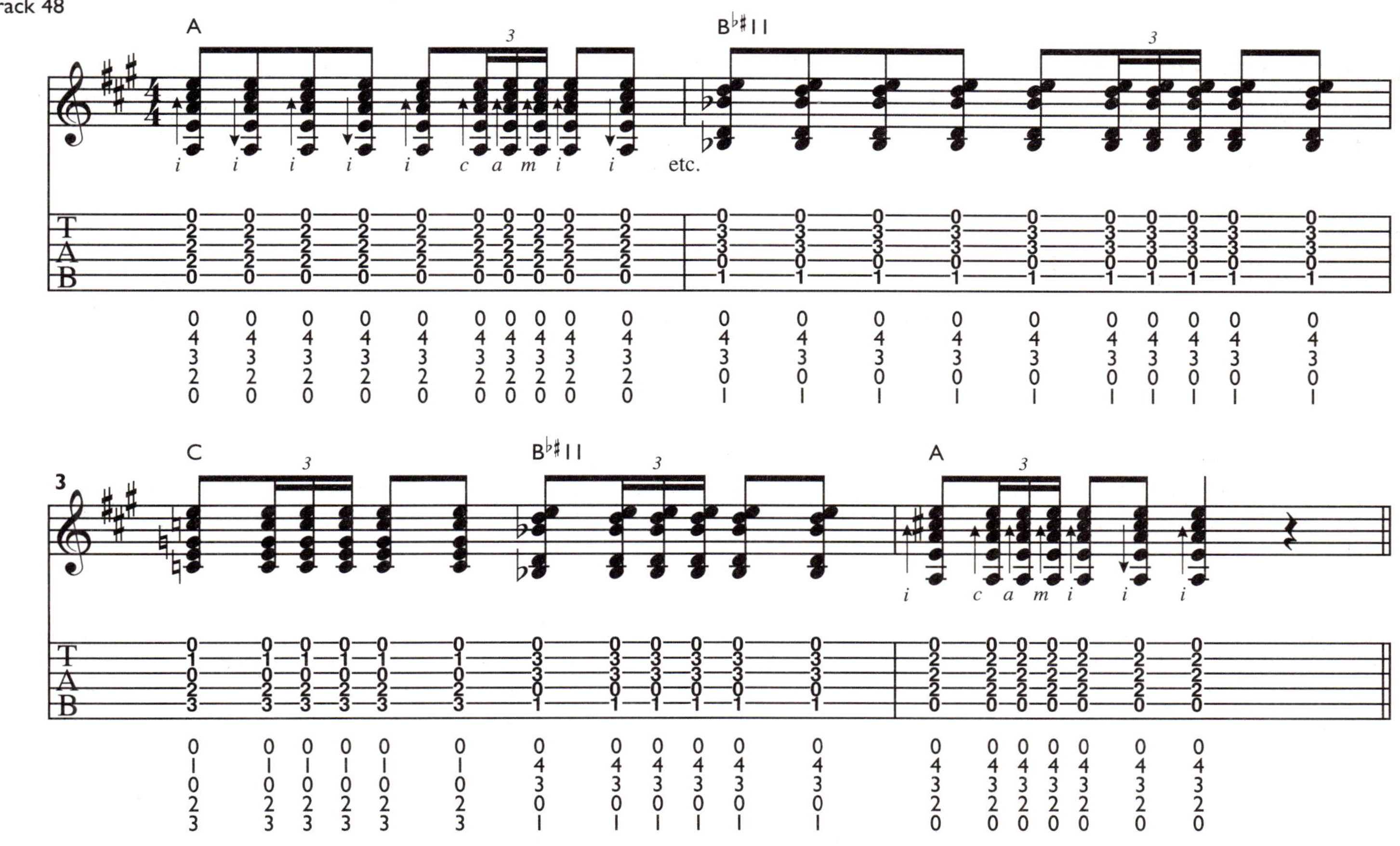

CHAPTER SEVEN
METAL AND SHRED GUITAR

++

Lesson 1: Metal Rhythm

In the early 1970s, bands like Black Sabbath and Deep Purple started to define the *heavy metal* sound. Who would have thought that today there would be many sub-genres of metal like thrash, death metal, progressive metal, and neo-classical speed metal, to name just a few. Of the crucial elements that tie these styles together, perhaps the most important factor is super-heavy guitar riffs played through tons of thick distortion.

Whether you are getting your distortion from an effects pedal, an overdriven amplifier, a rack unit, or a digital modeler, the main factor in getting a metal tone is to set your *gain* high. Once your signal is sufficiently distorted, you can further refine your tone by altering your EQ (equalization). In its simplest form, this would correspond to the bass, midrange (mids), and treble controls found on many amps. Turn your bass and treble controls up and your mids down, and you will get a deep, tight distortion similar to the sound made famous by bands like Metallica. This is known as "scooping your mids." Or, turn your midrange and treble up while keeping your bass down, and you will get a harsh distortion made famous by bands like Slayer. Other things that will contribute to a genuine metal tone are heavy picks, an aggressive pick attack, and a solid palm mute.

Once your tone is dialed in, try these examples. The first pattern starts off with palm-muted eighth-note downstrokes. Add alternate-strummed sixteenth notes and you've got a bread-and-butter metal technique known as the *gallop*. Then, continue with two galloping patterns built from triplets.

The Gallop

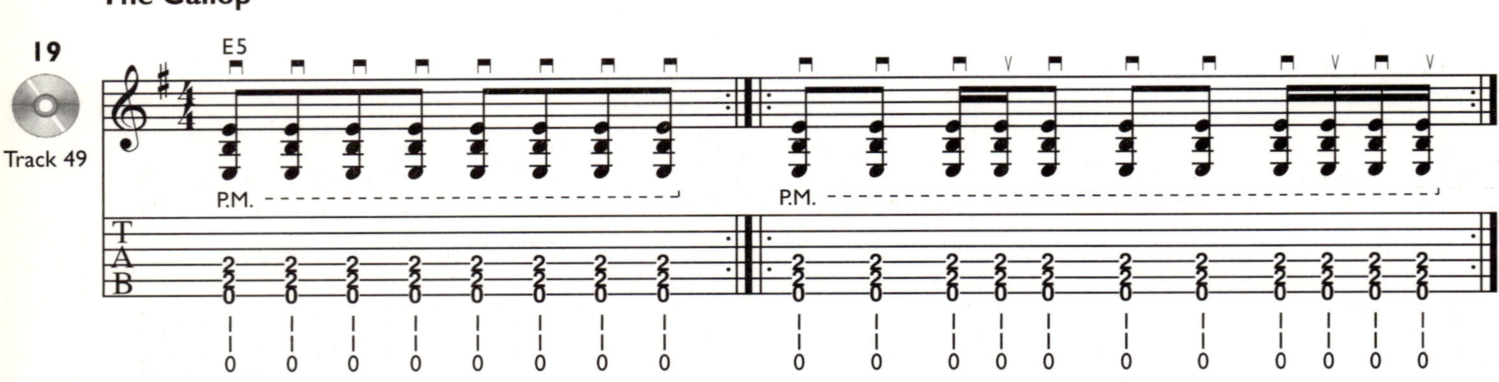

Triplet Gallop

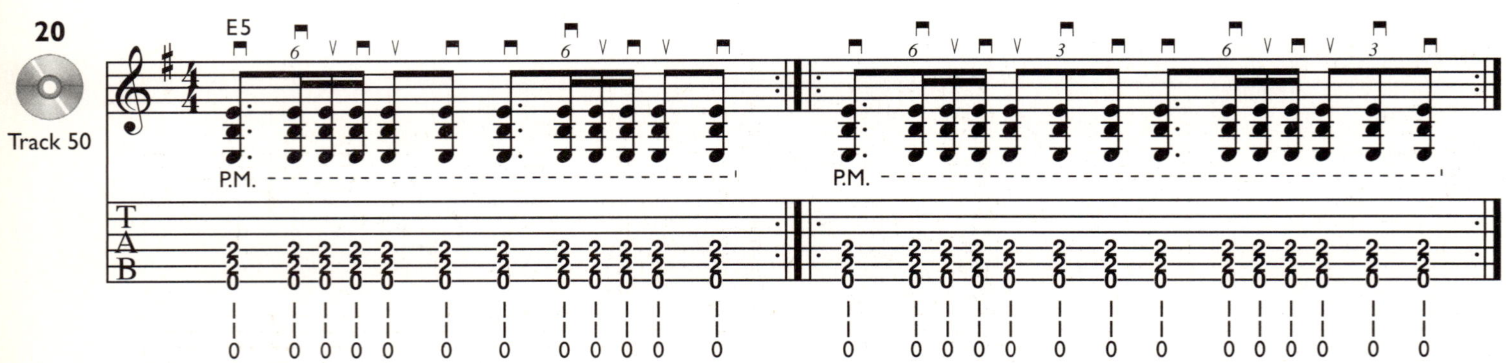

Following are examples in the styles of some popular metal artists. The first two patterns are based on the gallop. The second two examples are based on another useful rhythmic device: single-note melodic motifs that are interspersed with alternate picks of a pedal tone on the 6th string.

In the Style of Metallica

21 Track 51

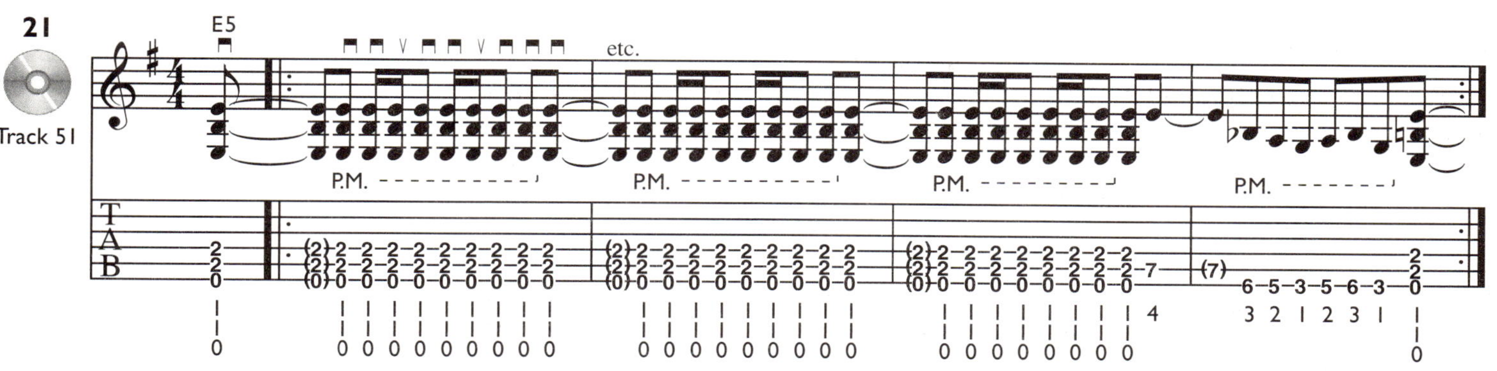

In the Style of Megadeth

22 Track 52

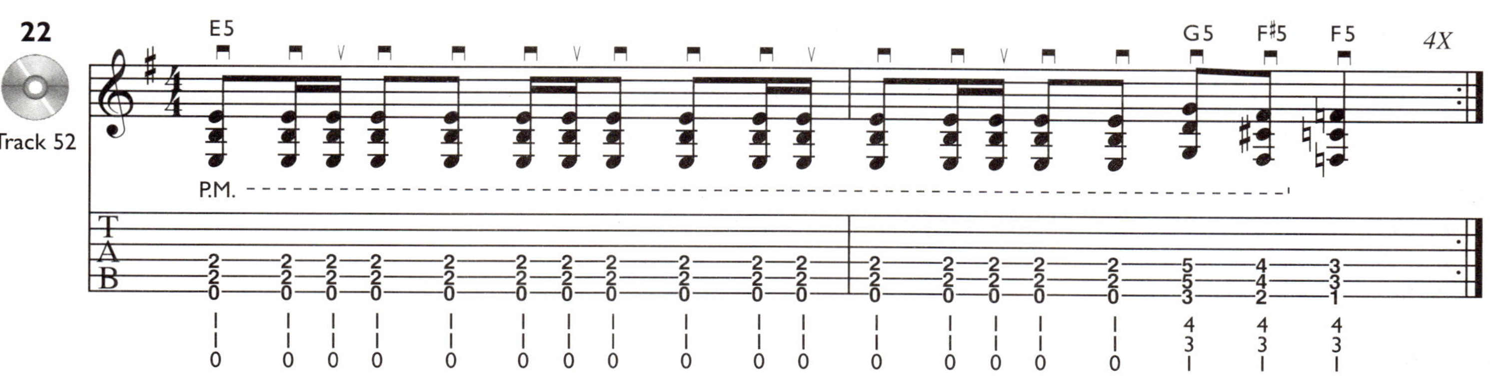

In the Style of Randy Rhoads

23 Track 53

In the Style of Slayer

24 Track 54

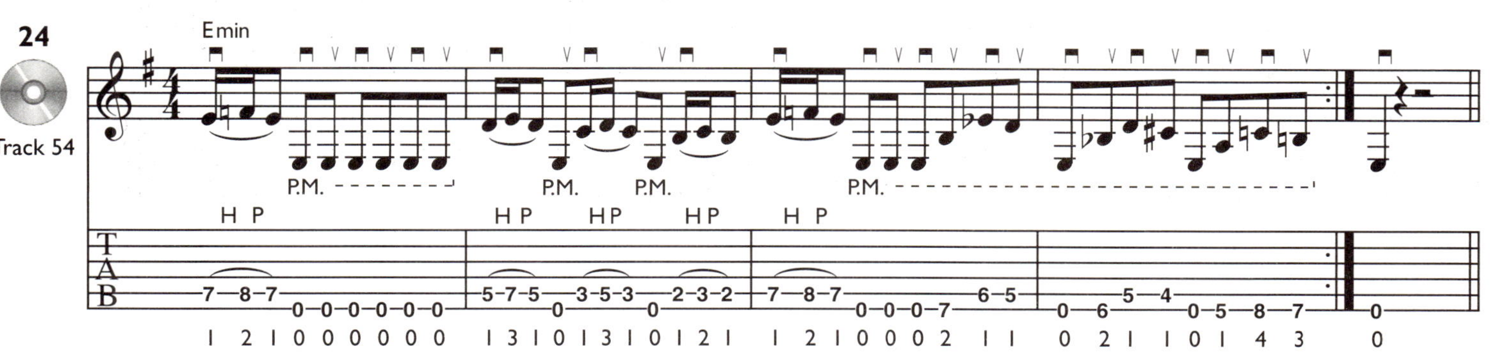

Lesson 2: Tremolo Picking

Tremolo picking is a crucial skill for the metal guitarist. It's a technique that usually involves targeting a single note with blisteringly fast alternate picking. One of the most effective ways to implement tremolo picking is to combine open-string picking with fretted notes, which is exactly what the following examples illustrate.

The first example, in the style of Iron Maiden, is based on the E Aeolian scale (illustrated below). With this riff, it's helpful to conceptualize the notes as a scale sequence. If you look closely, you'll see a diatonic pattern that can be boiled down to two steps down, one step up, two steps down, one step up, etc. Follow the arrows and you'll see the pattern.

The scale pattern and the tremolo picking can be thought of as two separate concepts which might be best practiced independently at first. For the tremolo picking, it's important to use a metronome to accurately practice at a slow speed on a single note. Gradually speed up as the timing and feel of the picking gets easier. A relatively light to medium grip on the pick is all you will need for effective tremolo picking. Separately, try the scale sequence below to get familiar with the notes. Then, combine the scale sequence with the tremolo picking, and you are ready for the riff below.

The E Aeolian Scale on One String

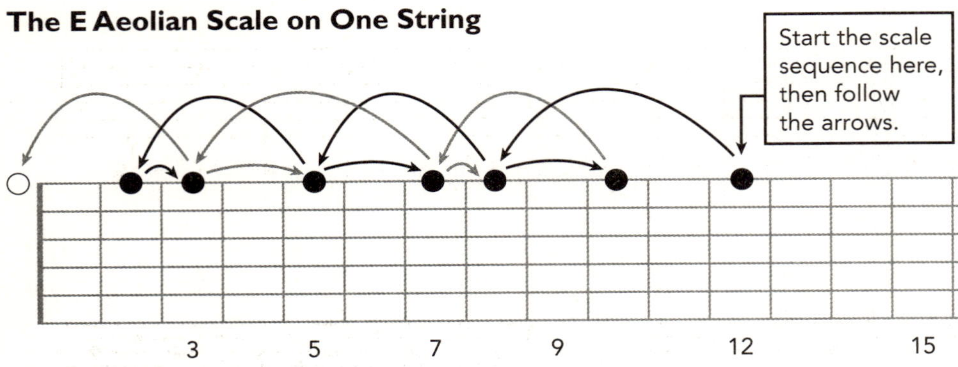

Tremolo Picking in the Style of Iron Maiden

    The Guitar Style Resource

Here's another tremolo picking example in the style of AC/DC's classic tune "Thunderstruck." AC/DC can be considered either hard rock or heavy metal, depending on whom you talk to. Regardless, their lead guitarist Angus Young has a mean tremolo-picking technique.

It's important to note that this example starts on an upstroke, rather than a downstroke, and then alternates fretted notes with open strings for the entire riff.

To truly master the art of tremolo picking, it's important to become comfortable with placing your downstrokes, as well as your upstrokes, on strong beats or weak beats. This example takes some serious coordination between the picking hand and the fretting hand, so make sure to start slowly.

In the Style of AC/DC

Lesson 3: Drop D and Odd-Time Riffs

How do you make a heavy riff even heavier? By retuning your guitar to drop D, of course. Many metal guitarists these days alter their guitar tuning from the standard E–A–D–G–B–E tuning to a heavier drop tuning. The simplest way to go into a drop tuning is to lower your 6th string by a whole step from E to D. Some will tune even lower by tuning to drop D, then lowering all six strings by a half step, or even a whole step (which would be a drop C tuning). Other metal guitarists achieve a similar heavy effect by using a seven-string guitar (a standard tuned guitar with an added low-B string). Besides the heavy sound, one of the benefits of playing a guitar tuned to drop D is that power chords can be played with a single barred finger. The example below is written in drop D and features single-finger power chords.

In the Style of Rage Against the Machine

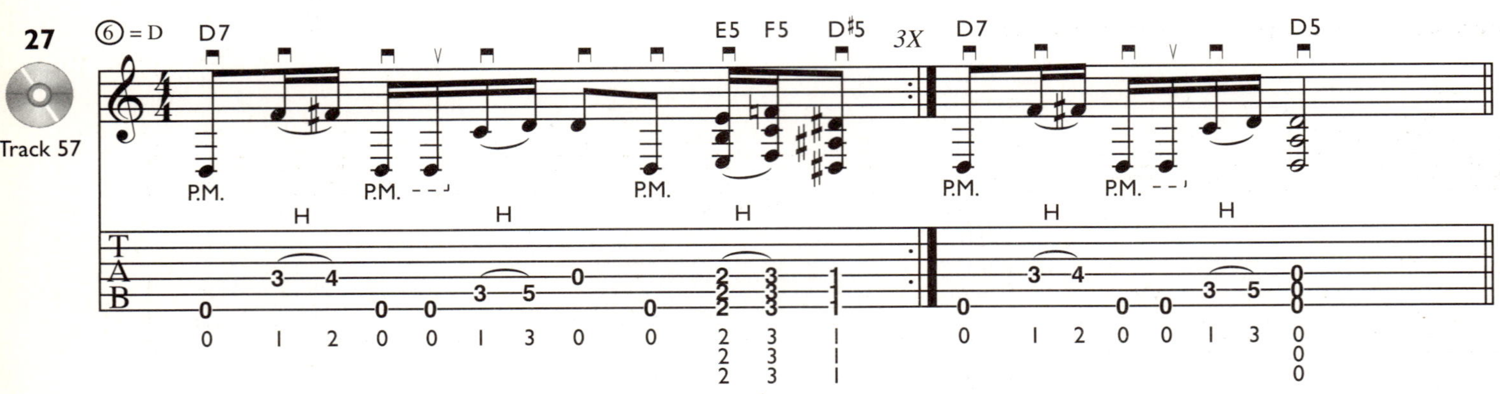

The next two examples are in drop D tuning, but they also feature a common characteristic found in many death metal and progressive metal tunes: *odd time signatures*. Odd time signatures are meters which don't fit in the common duple or triple categories like $\frac{4}{4}$ or $\frac{3}{4}$.

In the Style of Meshuggah

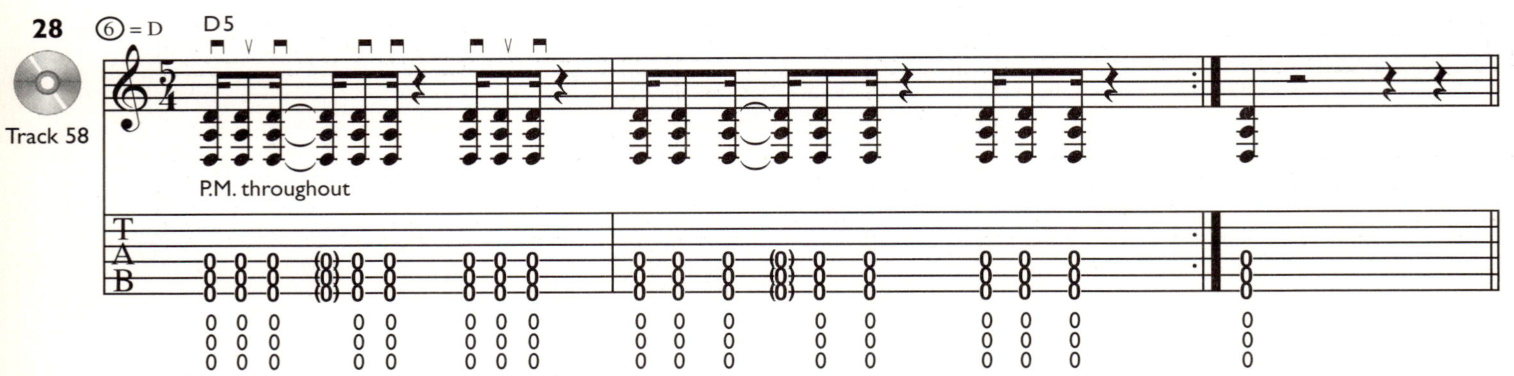

In the Style of Planet X

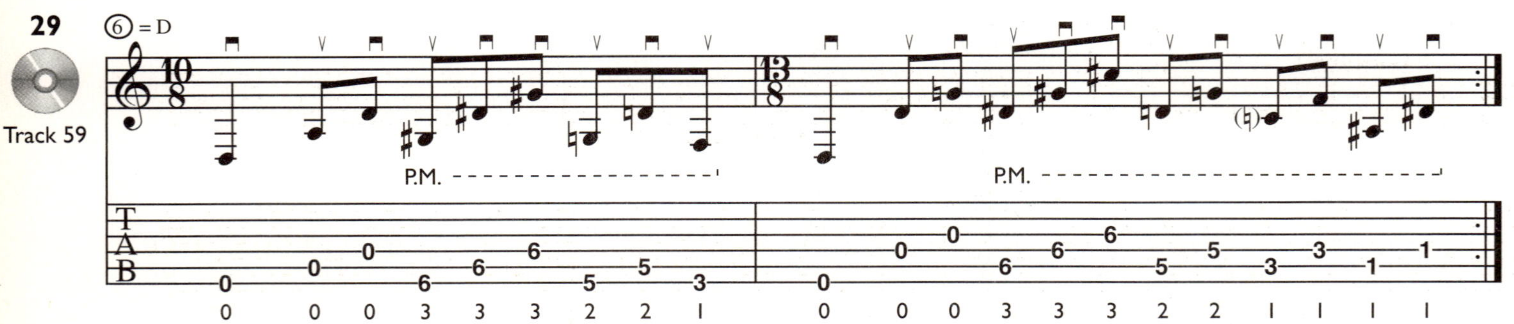

Lesson 4: Neo-Classical Metal

Neo-classical metal is a technically advanced style of guitar playing that is highly influenced by heavy metal and virtuosic classical music. Among the many devices used in neo-classical metal, one defining technique that stands out is *sweep picking*. Sweep picking usually involves playing *arpeggios* (the notes of a chord played separately rather than simultaneously) in such a way that the notes are rapidly picked in one fluid sweeping motion. The first example combines sweep picking with hammer-ons and pull-offs, the second example adds a *tap* (tapping is essentially a quick hammer-on and pull-off executed by a free finger in the picking hand), and the third example combines the first two arpeggio shapes with a 4th-finger slide. These examples illustrate three ways to sweep pick the same group of notes. Scale diagrams are provided to help you visualize the shapes.

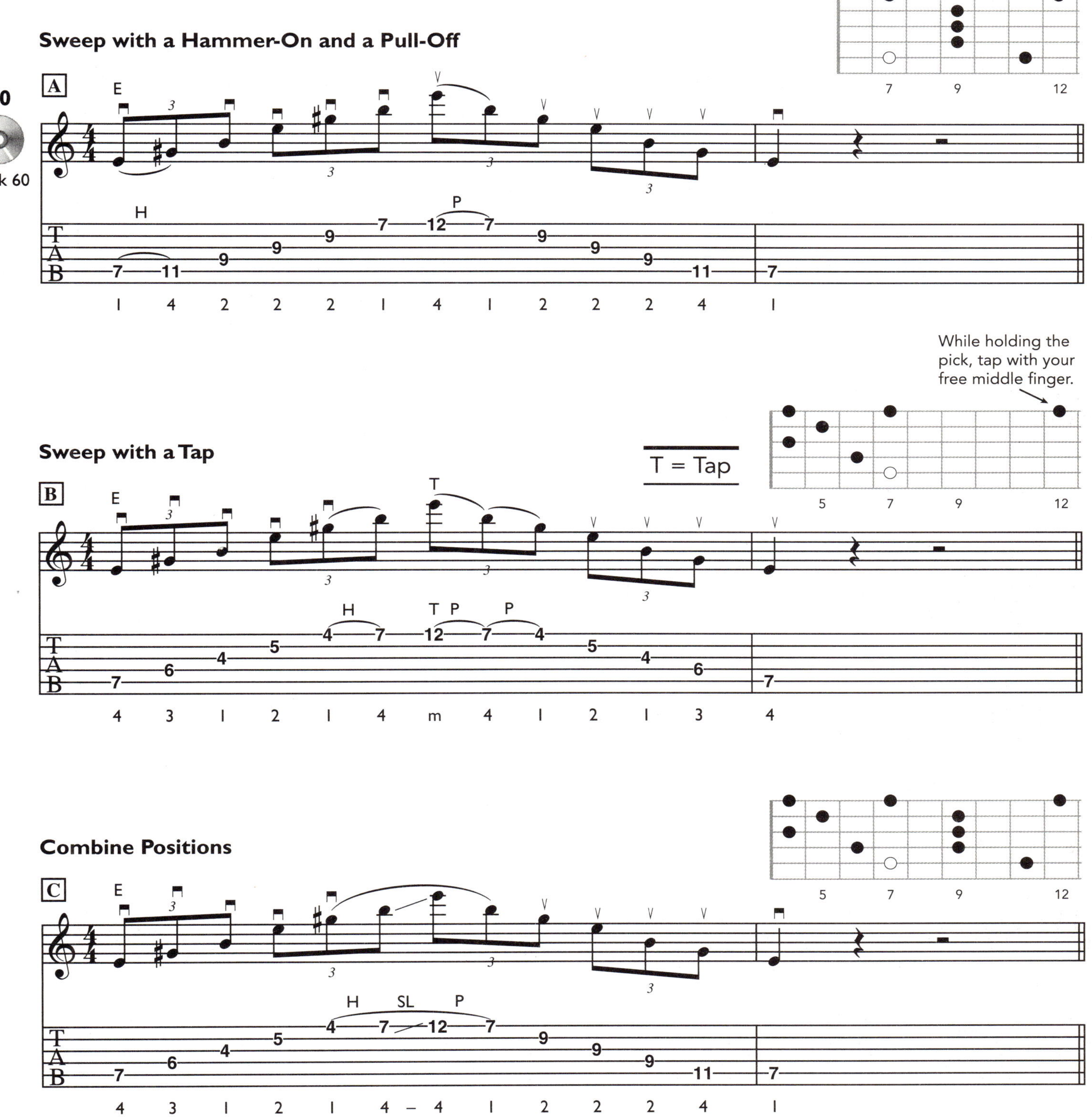

Here are the same sweep picking techniques applied over A Minor arpeggios. Feel free to combine these arpeggios with the E Major arpeggios on the previous page, and you are guaranteed to create some killer neo-classical sweep picking sequences.

With a Hammer-On and a Pull-Off

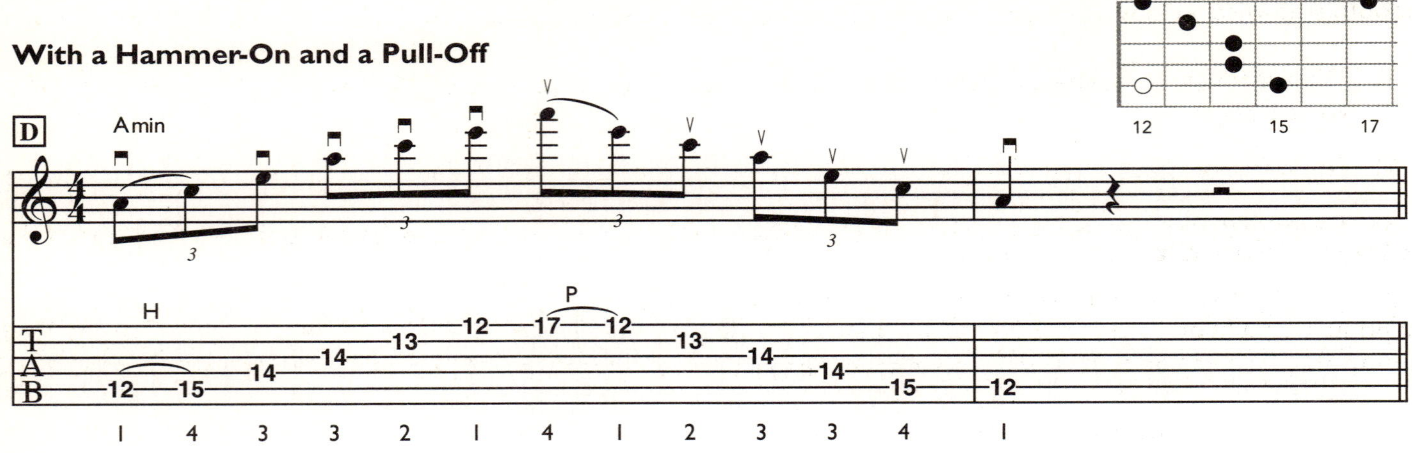

With a Tap

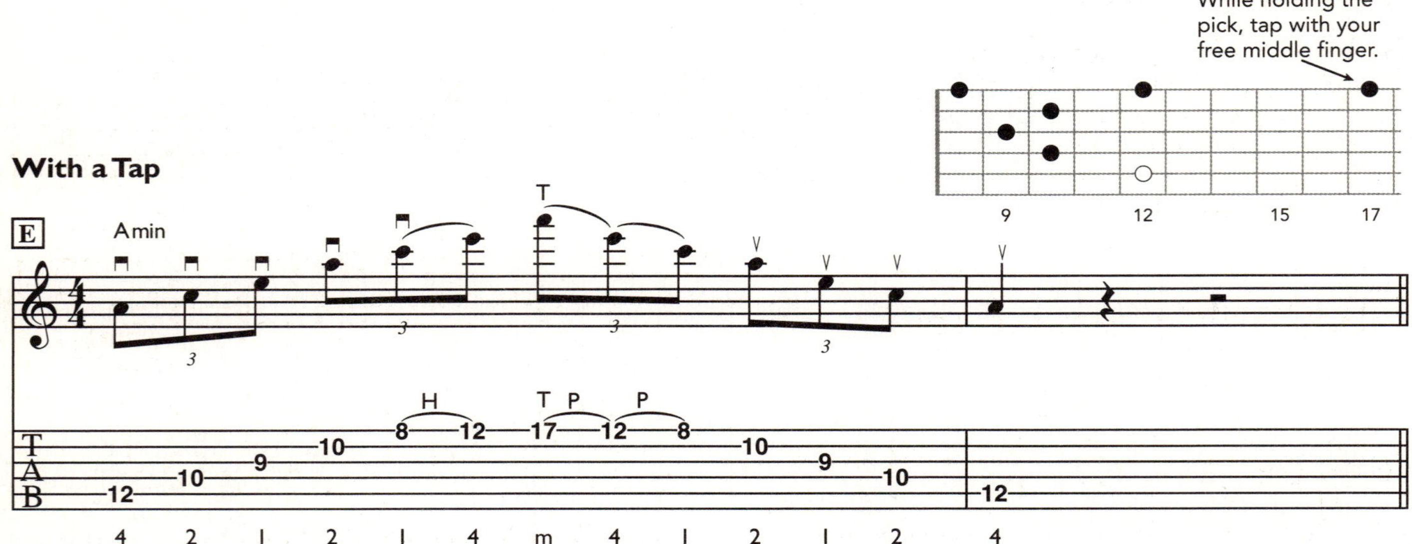

Combine Positions

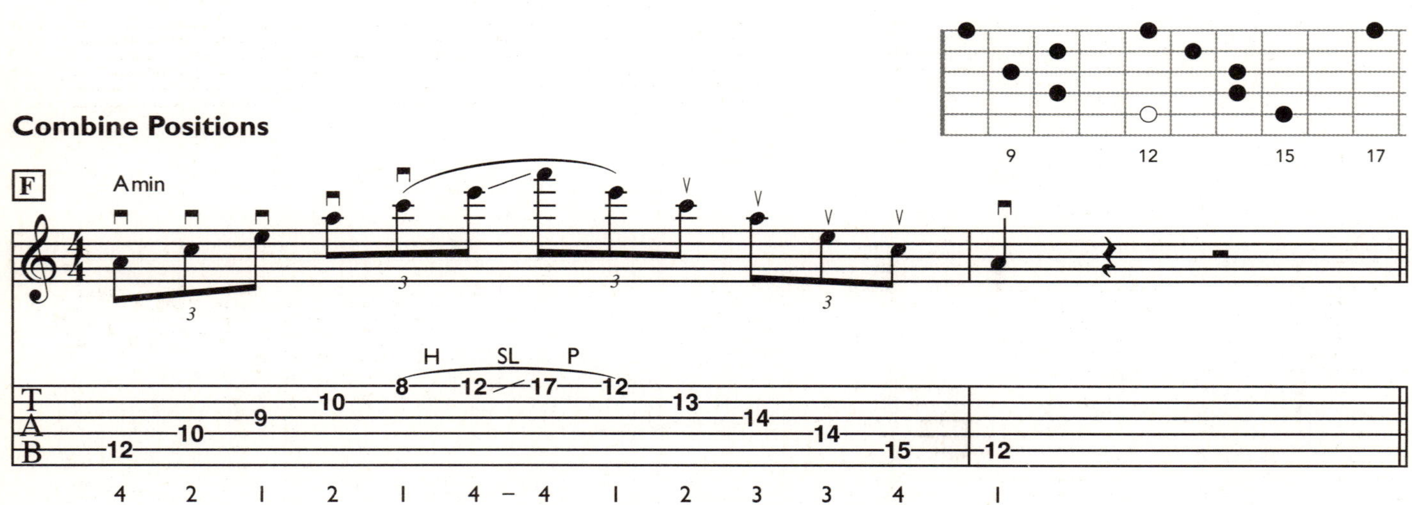

Get ready for a burning shred etude written in the style of the man who invented neo-classical metal, Yngwie Malmsteen. It starts off with some speedy tremolo picking on the 1st string, moves on to some crazy sweep picking arpeggios, and finishes with an Yngwie-style metal groove. Have fun with this one.

Malmsteen Madness

Track 61

Lesson 5: Shredding Tricks

Alternate picking involves maintaining a strict down–up–down–up pattern at all times. *Economy picking* is a cross between alternate picking and sweep picking (when switching to adjacent strings, sweep in the direction of the switch). Then, there's *hybrid picking*, which is a technique that involves using the pick and the fingers at the same time. In order to practice hybrid picking, try out this A Aeolian mode (one of metal's most used scales), visualized along the middle two strings. (For more on modes, see page 92.)

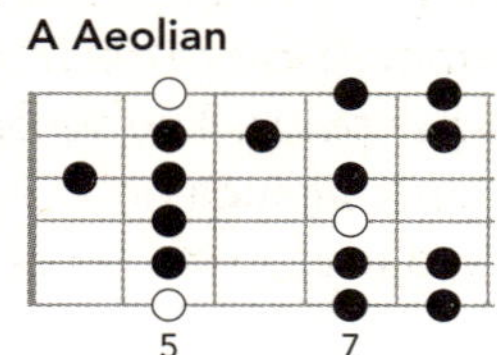

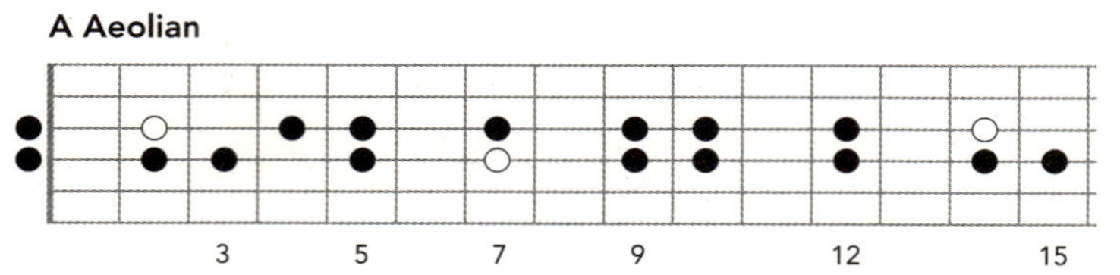

The A Aeolian mode can be played on six strings (above) or two strings (to the left).

Hybrid Picking

In the neo-classical metal genre, one of the most heavily used modes is the *harmonic minor scale*. To the right is a diagram illustrating the A Harmonic Minor scale in fifth position. Below is a fretboard pattern that works great in a harmonic minor context. It's connected with *legato* (smoothly played) hammer-ons. It was also used in the "Malmsteen Madness" tune on page 65.

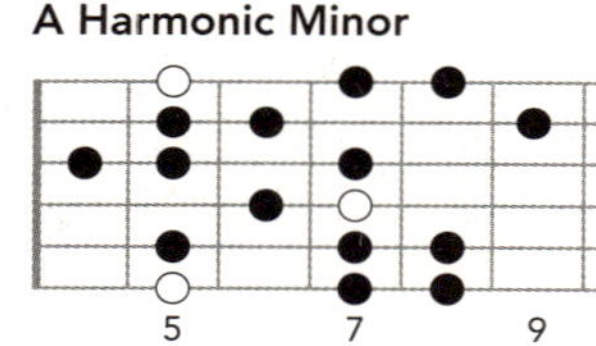

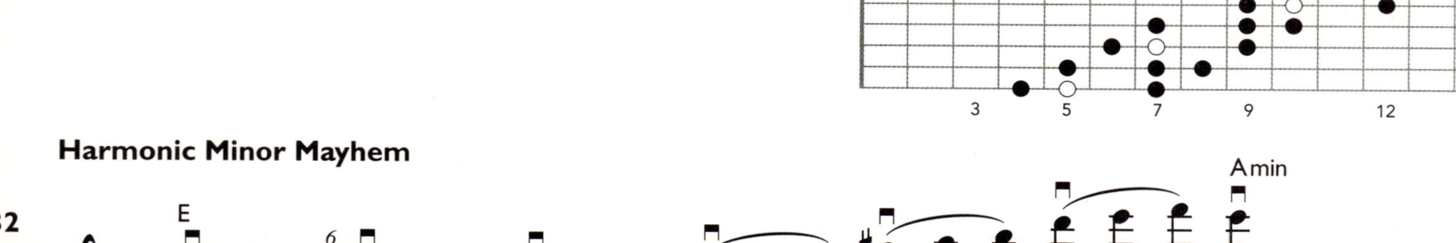

Harmonic Minor Mayhem

The next two examples are absolutely insane-sounding riffs in the style of ground-breaking shred guitarist Buckethead. They are shape-based riffs, meaning that, visually, they appear as symmetrical patterns on the fretboard. The first riff features tapping, hammer-ons, and string skipping. The second riff is a *circular* sweep picking pattern that zig-zags up and down the neck in such an efficient way that it can be played very quickly with ease. These are some burning riffs, so get ready to shred.

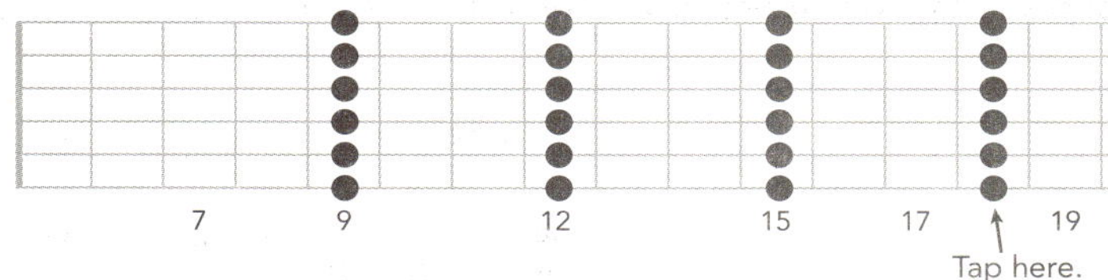

Tapping and Skipping

Circular Sweeping

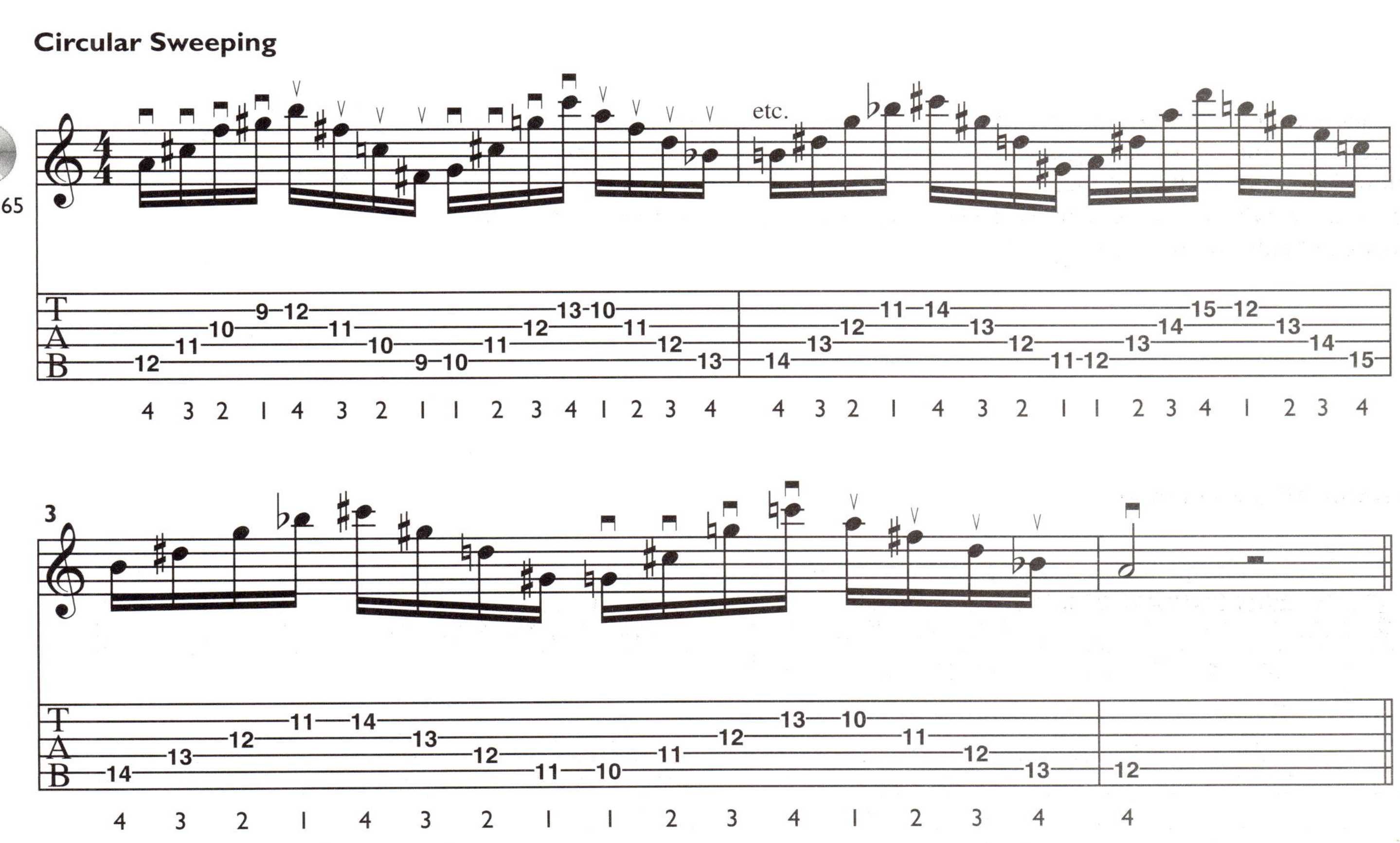

CHAPTER EIGHT
REGGAE AND SKA GUITAR

Lesson 1: Reggae Chord Voicings

Ska originated in Jamaica in the late 1950s through the blending of American rhythm and blues with traditional Jamaican music. Ten years later, *rocksteady* (a short-lived but very influential offshoot of ska) evolved into *reggae*. By the early 1970s, the success of Jamaican artist Bob Marley brought reggae's exposure to an international level, and reggae continues to be a popular musical style to this day.

Some of the best chord voicings to use with reggae are also used in rock (like the three- and four-note major chords illustrated on page 15). However, for a few of the upcoming reggae examples, you are going to need minor chords as well. To build them, use the diagram below, which illustrates an entire fretboard filled with a C Minor chord (which you can think of as the minor version of the CAGED system). Notice how this fretboard diagram can be split into five shapes, two of which are abbreviated to form some of the most common minor chords used in reggae. As you play these shapes, use the thumb and extraneous fingers in the fretting hand to mute out the lower strings.

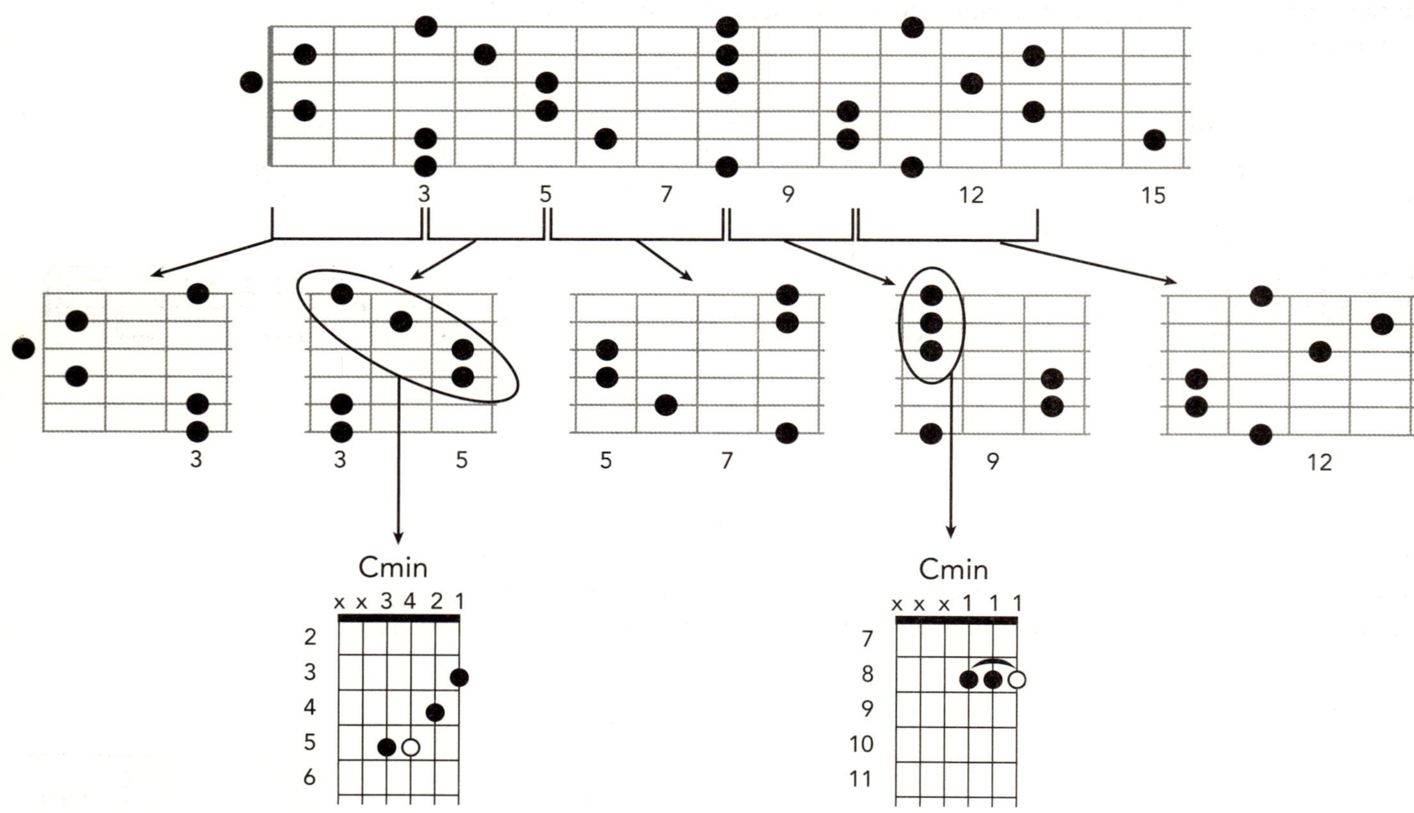

Lesson 2: Reggae Rhythm Chops

The guitar plays a primary role in creating the reggae sound. One of the most notable characteristics is the rhythm, which usually consists of short, choppy strums (also called *skanks*). These skanks are often placed on beats 2 and 4, but it's also common to see them as a set of two swung eighth notes starting on beats 2 and 4.

The first example is based on "Get Up, Stand Up" as played by Peter Tosh (the tune was actually co-written by Peter Tosh and Bob Marley). Like most reggae tunes, the chord progression is very simple. In this case, there's only a single chord in the whole tune. A strong palm mute on both the downstrokes and the upstrokes will help you achieve an authentic reggae sound.

The next example is in the style of the reggae classic "Stir It Up" by Bob Marley. It features the same rhythm as the previous tune, but adds a few choice reggae voicings. Keep that palm mute solid.

This next rhythm example is based on another Bob Marley classic, "Waiting in Vain." It features strums on beats 2 and 4 as expected. But it also includes a colorful major 7th chord and a *rake*. The rake is achieved by quickly scraping the pick from the low strings to the high strings while holding a palm mute. Listen to the audio track to get the timing just right.

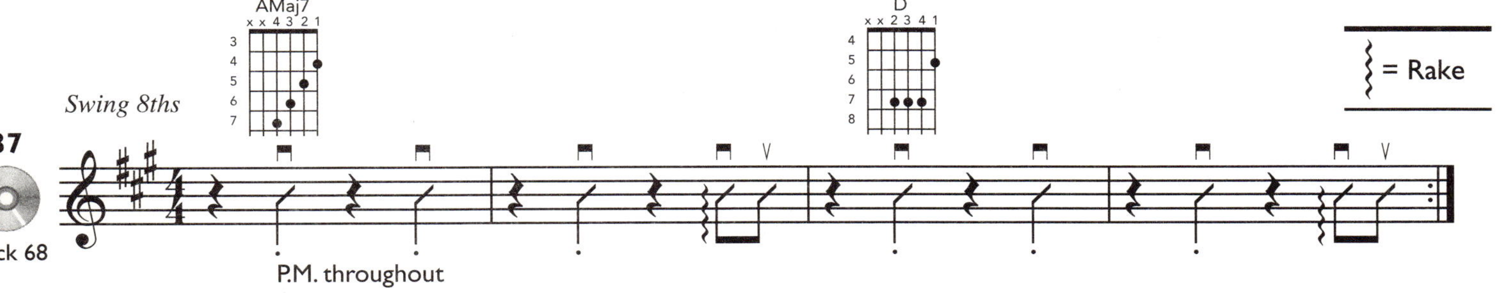

Lesson 3: Single-Note Syncopations

In reggae music, the rhythm guitar is not limited to just chord chops. In many reggae tunes, the rhythm guitar will play single-note riffs that compliment the bass and drums. These riffs will take many forms, depending on the individual song, but nearly all of them are very syncopated and almost always done with a heavy palm mute.

Example 38 is composed in the style of a classic tune called "Child of the Ghetto," written by Horace Andy, one of the original roots-reggae singers. Example 39 features single-note syncopations, and is in the style of Bob Marley's "Could You Be Loved." Example 40, which is in the style of "Black Wadada" by Burning Spear, shows how single-note melodies and chord chops can be combined into the same guitar part.

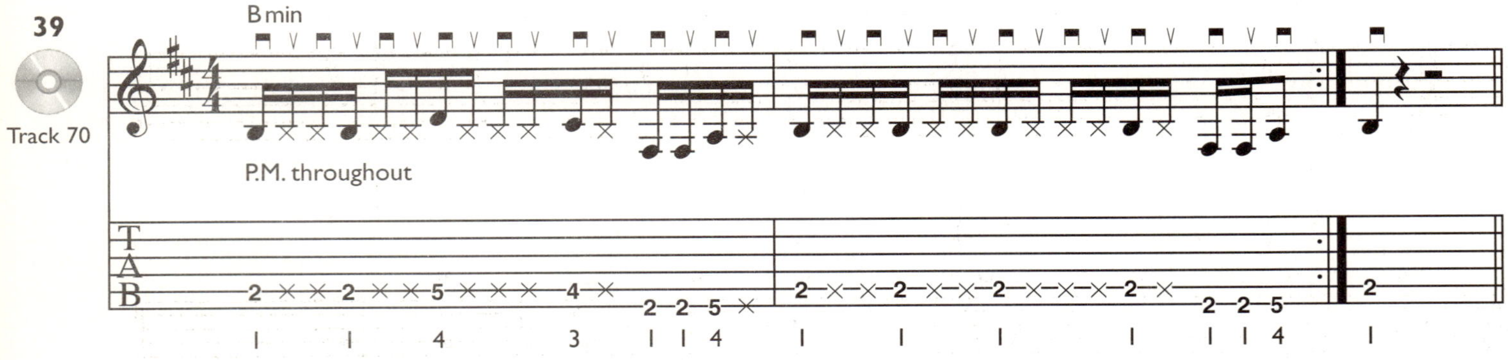

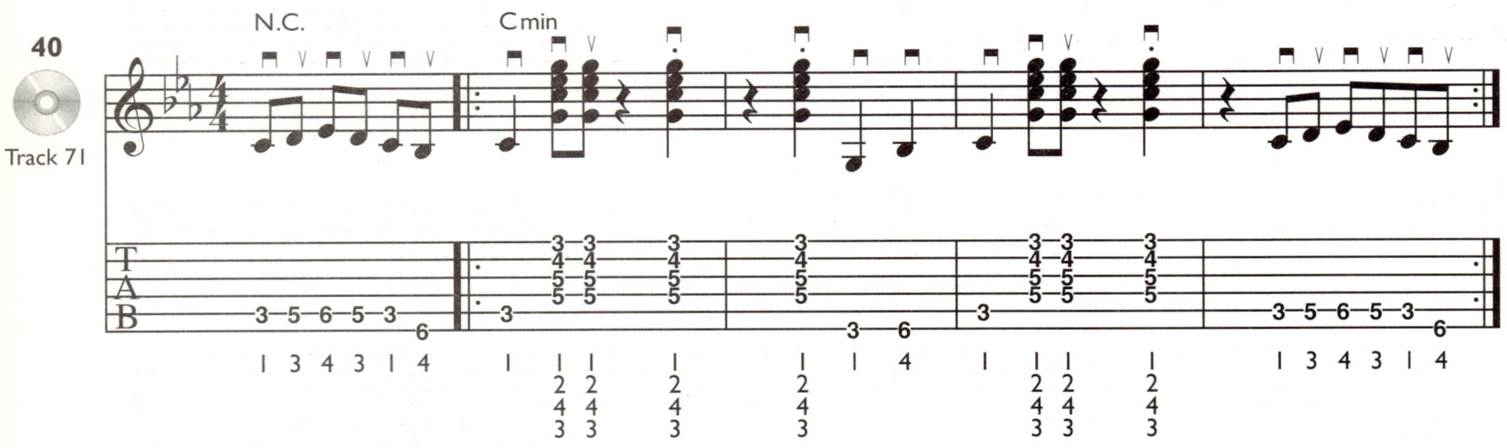

Here's a piece based on one of the most famous reggae tunes of all time, "I Shot the Sheriff" by Bob Marley. It combines all of the concepts covered so far in this chapter and adds a few more. The first section starts off with a single three-note G Minor chord played with a useful (yet less common) reggae rhythm. The second section features the classic eighth-note strum, but this time, it's only found starting on beat 2 (beat 4 is left out). The third section contains a syncopated single-note melody, and the last section is a repeat of the first section.

Rastafari Police

Track 72

Lesson 4: Third Wave Ska

In the early 1960s, ska was the dominant musical style in Jamaica. By the time the late '60s had rolled around, ska had already been replaced by rocksteady and reggae. It wasn't until the late 70s that ska enjoyed a punk-influenced resurgence in England called the *2 Tone movement* (named after the 2 Tone Records label).

A few years later, bands which were influenced by the 2 Tone sound began to form in the United States. This is known as ska's *third wave*, which is still an active movement today. Third wave ska is the focus of this entire lesson, starting with an example in the style of New York ska legends the Toasters. The second example is in the style of Less Than Jake, which is followed by an example in the style of the Mighty Mighty Bosstones. Get ready for some serious offbeat upstrums, the trademark of this style.

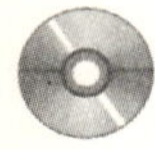
Don't Come Toasting

Track 73

More Than Inspired

Track 74

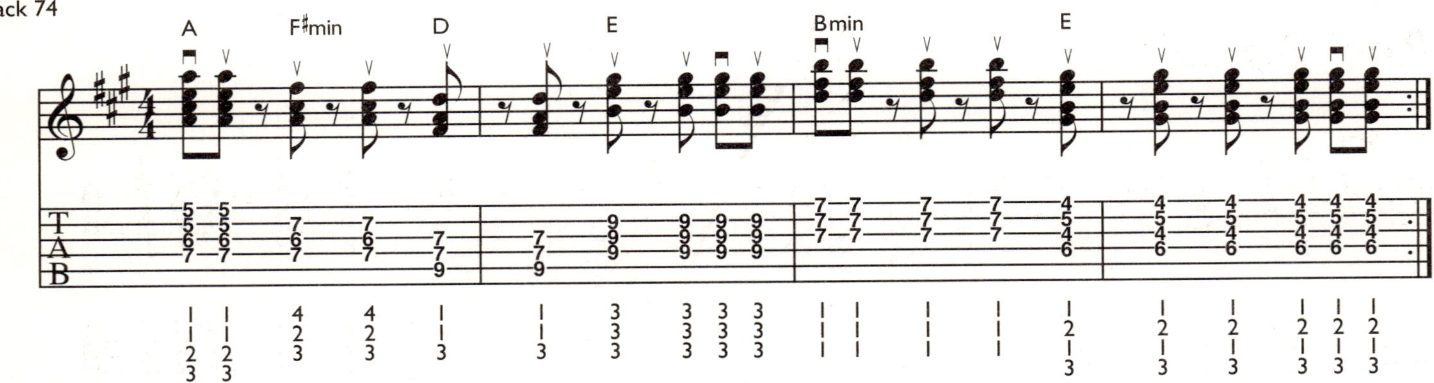

Dr. Bosstone

Track 75

The final two examples illustrate a few of the stylistic variations commonly seen in third wave ska. "Sub-lime" is based on Sublime's hit tune "Santeria," and "Reel Big Sale" is based on the tune "Sell Out" by the popular ska-punk band Reel Big Fish. Notice how the first example features chord arpeggios, and the second example includes some heavy punk-influenced distortion.

Sub-Lime

Track 76

Reel Big Sale

Track 77

CHAPTER NINE
FUNK GUITAR

Lesson 1: Single-Note Funk Lines

In the mid-to-late 1960s, soul, R&B, and jazz styles started to blend, forming what we now know as *funk*. Funk musicians did away with the complex harmony found in jazz and soul, kept some of the spicy chord voicings, and emphasized the bass and drums. These changes resulted in a rhythmically-oriented style that was very influential to many other musical genres, such as disco, hip-hop, and jam bands. In funk styles, the guitar plays an important role by integrating syncopated, interlocking rhythm riffs with the bass and drums. This lesson illustrates the types of single-note lines that you are likely to come across in the funk genre. In the first example, the eighth notes are played in a staccato fashion. In other words, they should be played with an abrupt, non-sustaining attack, creating a sharp, funky sound.

In the Style of Wild Cherry

In the Style of Sly & the Family Stone

The tune below is in the style of the legendary New Orleans funk band the Meters. It illustrates how syncopated single-note lines can be combined with staccato chord chops. Funk chord voicings often consist of only two or three notes and are usually placed on the higher string sets. Also, take special notice of the muted *scratches* appearing in the first section right before the chords. This key funk technique is done by placing the fret-hand fingers on the strings as you strum (without fretting them), thereby creating a fret-hand mute, not a palm mute. Have fun grooving with this funky tune.

Funky Strut

Track 80

Lesson 2: The Chicken Scratch

One of the characteristic sounds of funk guitar is known as the *chicken scratch*. It's a technique for strumming chords that was pioneered by Jimmy Nolen, who was best known for playing guitar in James Brown's band.

As you strum, lightly squeeze the chord shape with your fretting hand, then immediately lift off the pressure so that the chord rings only for an instant. This creates a sharp scratch of a chord strum that can only be described as funky. Try this technique with the following tune, based on the brilliantly sparse riff for "I Feel Good" by James Brown.

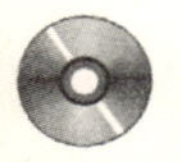

Feeling Funky

Track 81

Lesson 3: Building Chord Extensions

What makes funk so funky? Well, rhythm certainly plays a big part in creating a funky sound. But another important aspect has to do with the chord voicings that funk guitarists use. Funk chord voicings are sometimes made up of simple two- and three-note major and minor triads or dominant 7th chords. However, the chords that most clearly define the funk sound are voicings that include *extensions* (these are also called *tensions*).

Extensions are *compound* intervals (intervals greater than an octave) that are added to the primary chord tones of a voicing in order to add color to the chord. It's one thing to memorize the names and shapes of these extended chords, but it's also important to learn how to build them. The following diagrams illustrate how to do this.

1) Before building chord extensions, it's important to know how to locate and identify compound intervals. In order to do this, start with a common one-octave major scale:

4) Before adding the compound intervals to the primary chord tones, let's review basic chord construction (covered on page 10). Put the 1st (root), 3rd, and 5th together and you have a basic major triad.

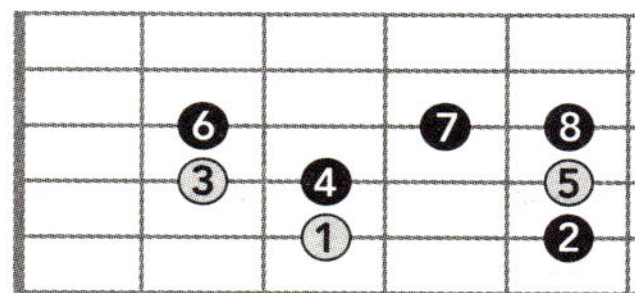

2) Look closely at this major scale. It's important to realize that the 1st scale degree and the 8th scale degree are the same note, separated by an octave. This means the 8th scale degree could be called either 1 or 8.

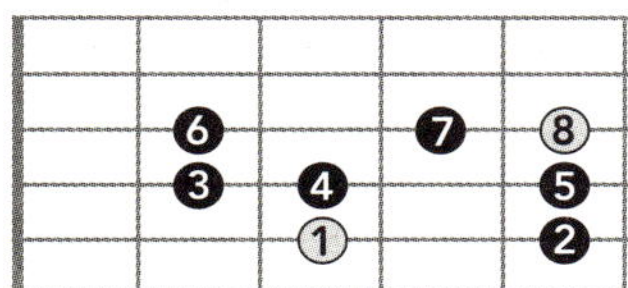

5) Add the 7th to the 1st, 3rd, and 5th, and you have identified the scale degrees of a major 7th chord. These four chord tones can be arranged in many different formations to form a variety of voicings, and the scale degrees can be altered to form different types of chords.

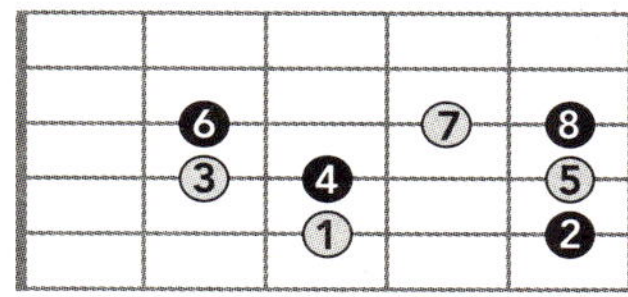

3) Using the same logic, if you travel up the major scale beyond the octave, you could call the 2nd scale degree a 9th, the 3rd scale degree a 10th, and so on. In a nutshell, the best way to identify compound intervals is to add the number 7 to any given *simple* interval. Here's the full set:

$$\text{Simple intervals}\begin{bmatrix} 8 & + & 7 & = & 15 \\ 7 & + & 7 & = & 14 \\ 6 & + & 7 & = & 13 \\ 5 & + & 7 & = & 12 \\ 4 & + & 7 & = & 11 \\ 3 & + & 7 & = & 10 \\ 2 & + & 7 & = & 9 \\ 1 & + & 7 & = & 8 \end{bmatrix}\text{Compound intervals}$$

6) Now that the 1st, 3rd, 5th, and 7th have been identified, take a look at the scale degrees between the primary chord tones. These intervals are the extensions. As the diagram below illustrates, they are named as compound intervals: 9, 11, and 13. These extensions add color and spice to simple triads and 7th chords.

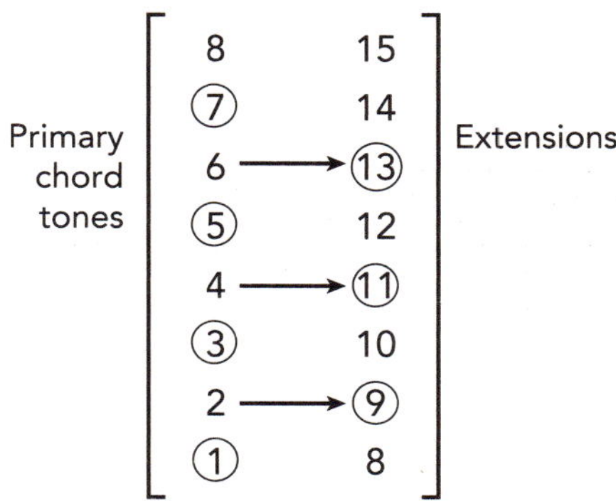

Now that chord extensions have been explained, let's put them to use in a funk context. Even though extensions can be altered just like primary chord tones, funk styles commonly stick to chords that add the 9th and/or the 13th. Keeping this in mind, here are some important funk voicings that include 9ths and 13ths.

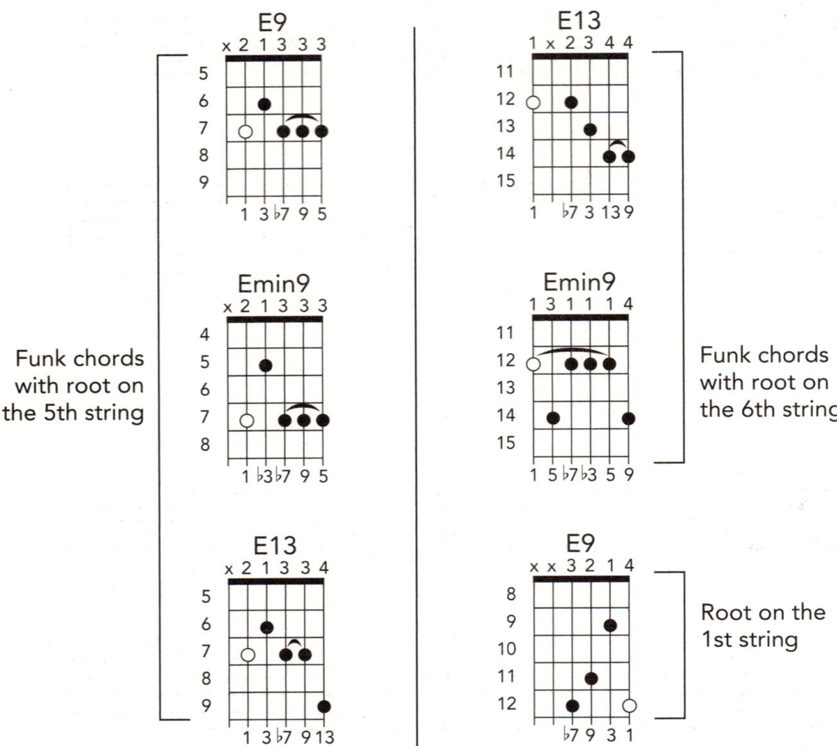

Lesson 4: Funky Rhythm Guitar

The following examples all feature chords that include 9ths and 13ths. The tunes also make good use of a bread and butter funk technique: sixteenth-note chord strumming. The first example is in the style of a classic funk tune called "Love Rollercoaster" by the Ohio Players. The second example is based on one of the most famous funk tunes ever written, "Papa's Got a Brand New Bag" by James Brown. As you play these tunes, try switching your pickup selector to the bridge or treble side for an extra-snappy tone.

Theme Park Funk

Track 82

Bag of Potatoes

The following two examples are based on tunes recorded in 1970 by the godfather of soul, James Brown. These examples contain plenty of spicy chords, slick sixteenth-note strumming (keep your wrist loose when you strum those sixteenth notes), and some serious fret-hand muting. Get ready to get your groove on with these funky riffs.

Funk Machine

Track 84

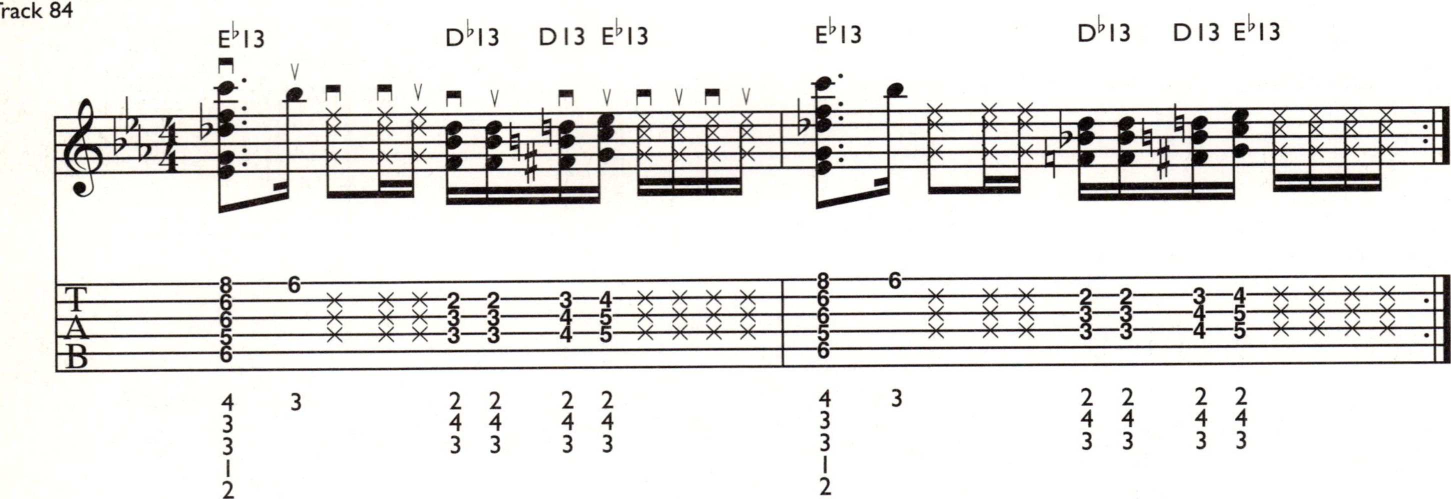

Super Funky

Track 85

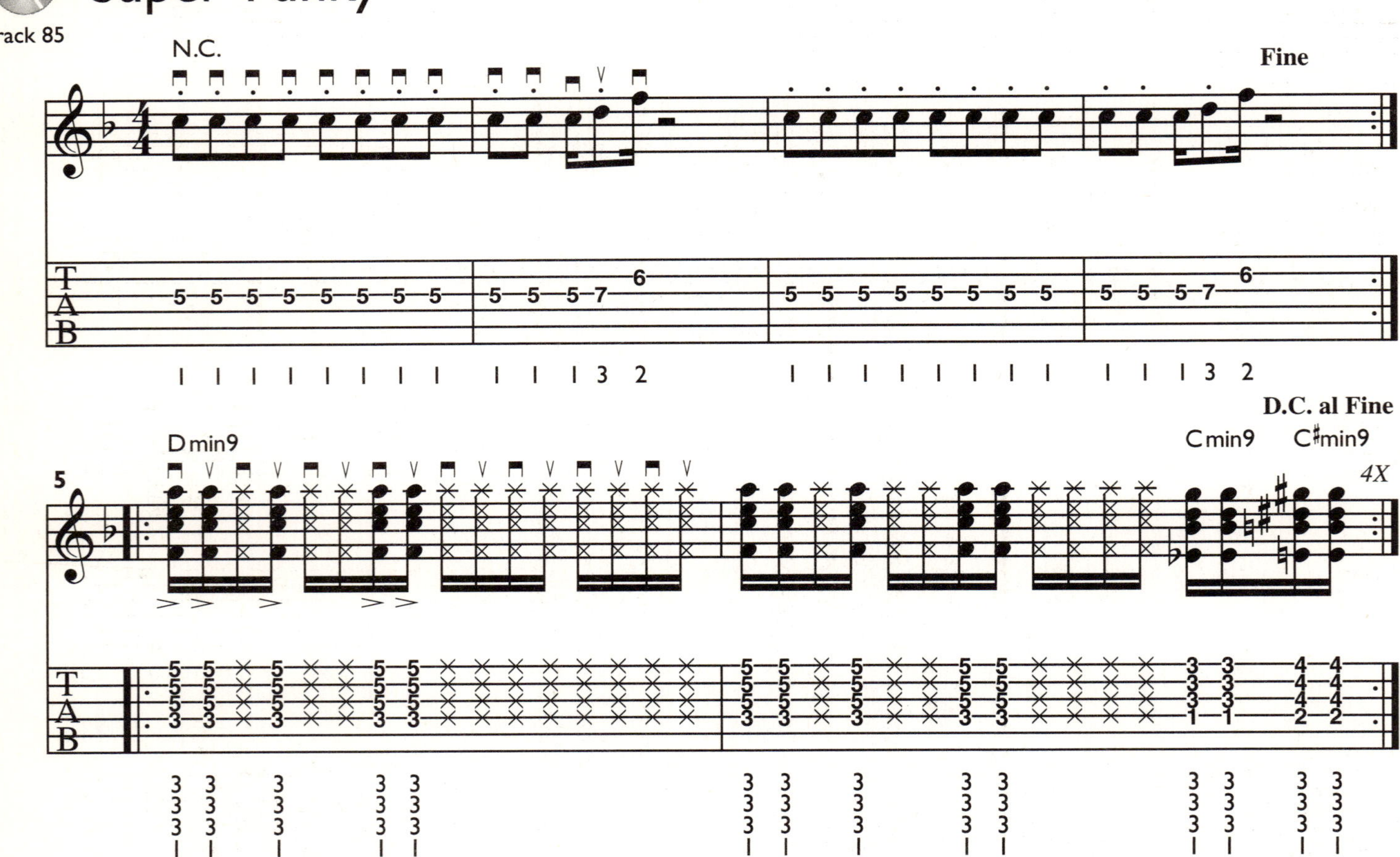

Note about soloing: Soloing in a funk style is heavily influenced by rock and blues guitar licks (covered on pages 21, 22, 31, and 32). However, a distinct characteristic of the funk genre is that the tunes are almost exclusively written in the Mixolydian or Dorian modes. Experiment with the rock and blues licks, along with the Mixolydian and Dorian modes (see page 92), while improvising over the tunes in this chapter.

CHAPTER TEN
JAZZ GUITAR

+ +

Lesson 1: Jazz Chord Progressions

The guitar has a rich and varied history within the jazz tradition. During the late 1930s and early 1940s, the jazz guitar was purely an instrument for rhythmic accompaniment. But, thanks to virtuosic pioneers like Charlie Christian, Wes Montgomery, and many others, the guitar soon came to be respected as a lead instrument as well. Before exploring the intricacies of jazz guitar, it's important to understand jazz harmony, which at its essence comes from 7th chords. Below is a diagram that illustrates how to build 7th chords and how they function.

Step 1) Start with the harmonized major scale illustrated on page 23:

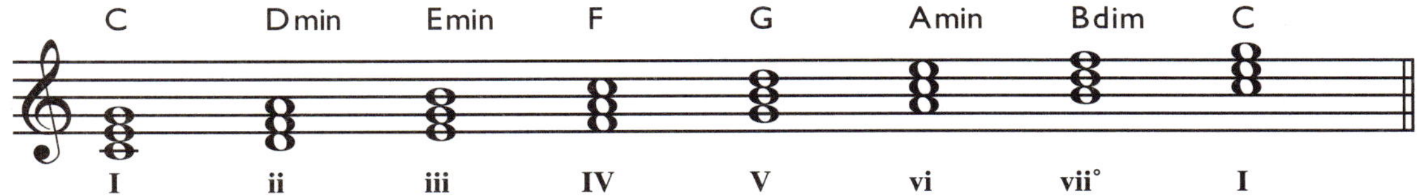

Step 2) Stack a diatonic 3rd above the 5th in each triad. You end up with a
sequence of 7th chords:

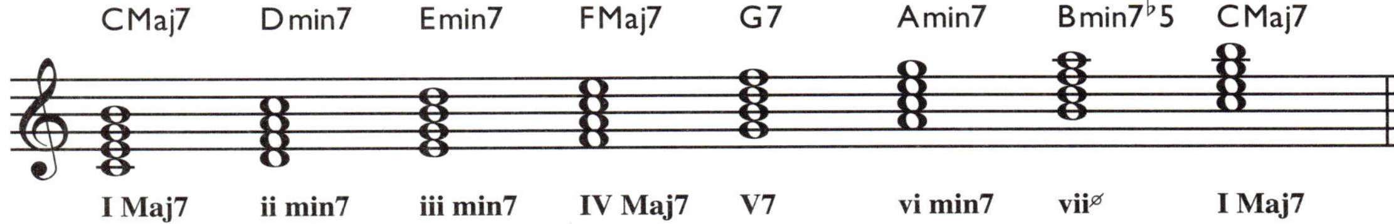

One of the most common chord sequences found in jazz is the ii–V–I chord progression. By referring to the diagram above, it's clear that a ii–V–I in the key of C would be: Dmin7–G7–CMaj7. Check out the following chord voicings to get a feel for this quintessential jazz progression:

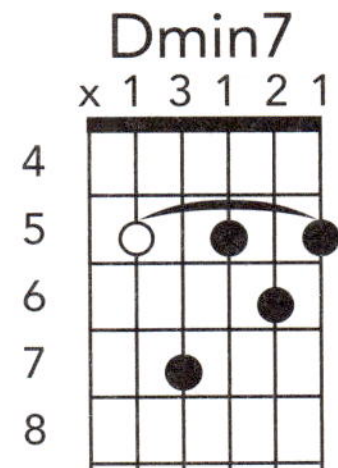

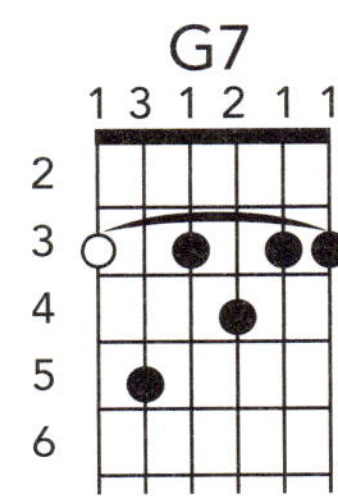

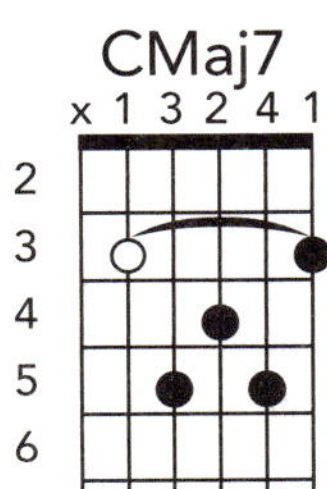

Jazz composers often use ii–V–I progressions as a harmonic device for establishing new key centers. This technique is illustrated in the following example based on the 1940 jazz standard "How High the Moon," written by Morgan Lewis. The voicings introduced on the previous page are used exclusively, and harmonic analysis is included. Try strumming the chords with your thumb to get a mellow sound.

How New the Key

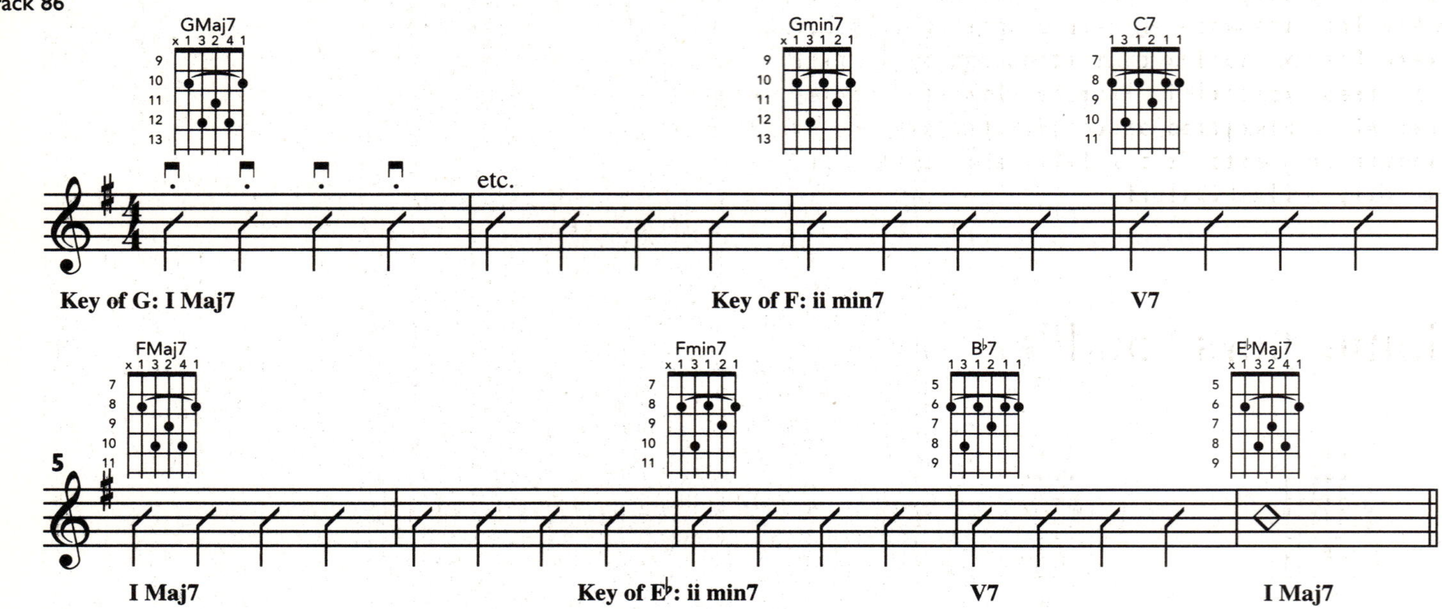

The next example is in the style of John Lewis's 1949 jazz standard "Afternoon in Paris." As with the previous example, this tune is chock full of ii–V–I progressions. However, the harmonic rhythm (the rate at which the chords change) has been doubled. Also, notice how an accent has been added on beats 2 and 4 in order to enhance the swing feel of this "four-to-the-bar" rhythm style made famous by big band jazz guitar master Freddie Green. Three new chord voicings are introduced as well; see if you can find them.

Chords in the Afternoon

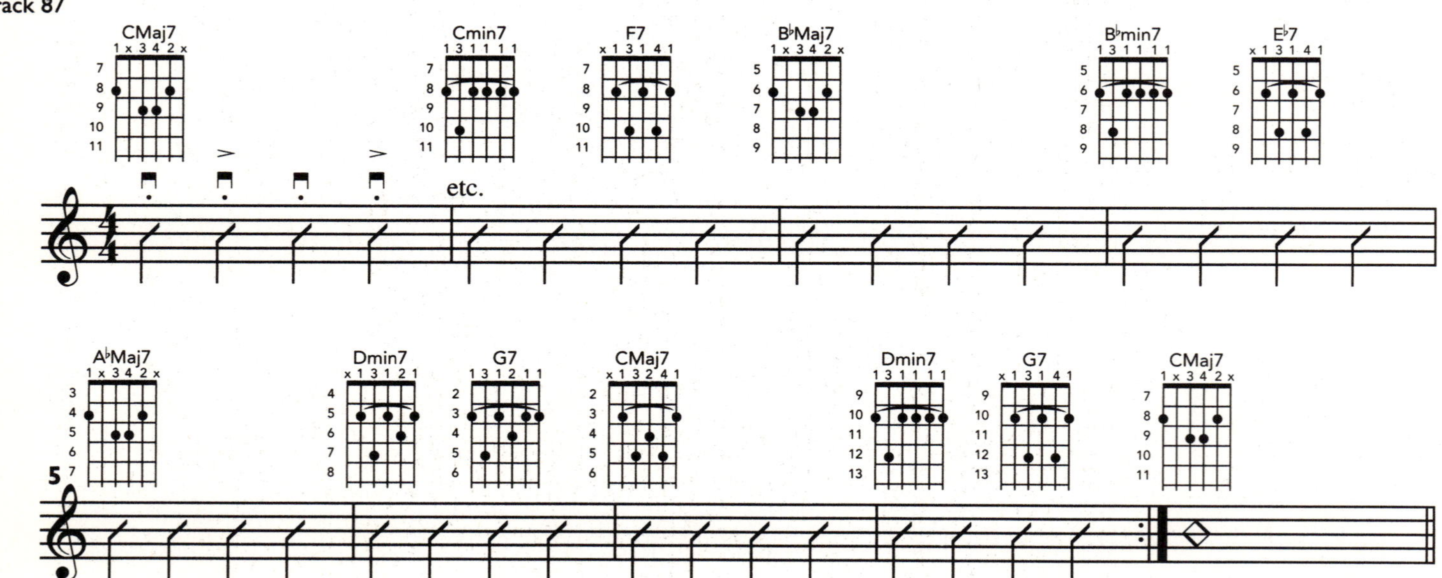

Chord progressions that follow the *cycle of 5ths* are a common trait in standard jazz repertoire, as well as in other styles of music. To see how this works, take a look at the song below in the style of the 1939 classic "All the Things You Are" by Jerome Kern.

As the diagram to the right illustrates, the first five chords of the tune feature root movement counterclockwise around the cycle of 5ths, while the chords themselves are all diatonic to the key of A♭ (starting on the vi min7 chord). This sequence is followed by a quick ii–V–I in a new key. Then, the whole eight-bar progression is repeated in two new keys. The six chord voicings introduced on the previous two pages are used exclusively in this tune. However, they are sparsely executed with a syncopated jazz *comping* style (comping is short for "accompaniment") epitomized by bebop and hard-bop piano greats Wynton Kelly and Red Garland.

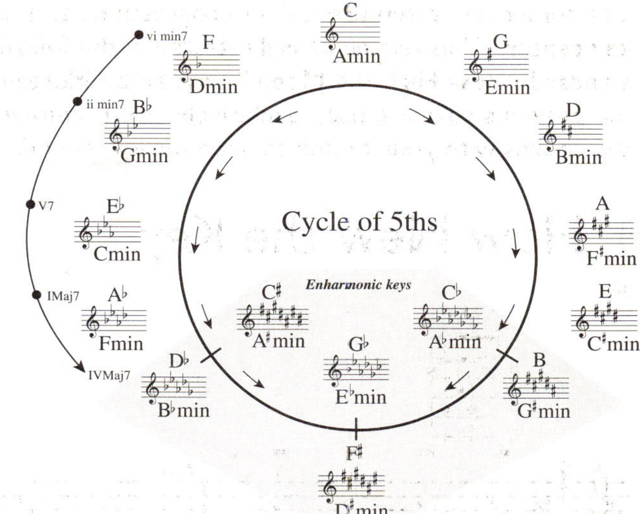

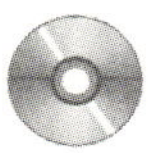

Some Keys You Play

Track 88

Swing 8ths

Lesson 2: Soloing Over ii-V-I Progressions

The examples on this page illustrate two different strategies for soloing over ii–V–I
progressions. The first example is constructed from a stepwise scale pattern played in a
linear fashion up and down the key of C. In this case, the first note of each measure starts
on a chord tone, which helps outline the chord changes. The second example is constructed
from chord arpeggios, and the third example is a combination of both approaches. The last
example is the most sophisticated of the three, because the chord changes are made up
of ii–V–I progressions in three different keys. In addition, the last example features added
rhythmic variation and a quicker harmonic rhythm.

Linear Soloing

Lesson 3: Jazz Blues & Walking Bass

What do you get when you take a basic 12-bar blues form, modify the rhythm with jazz phrasing, and alter the harmony with jazzy chord substitutions? A *jazz blues*, of course. In the following jazz blues example, the dominant 7th chords (of which only two shapes are used) are played not only as I, IV, and V chords, but also as III, VI, and II chords, creating a sophisticated jazz sound. Furthermore, these voicings are linked by a *walking bass line* that adds an authentic jazz feel to the progression while creating the illusion of two parts being played simultaneously. In order to maintain separation between the chords and the bass line, a fingerstyle technique might work best (using the thumb for the bass line and fingers for the rest), but a hybrid technique using pick and fingers would work as well. Congratulations, you are now your own bass player!

Bop Blues Stroll

Track 90

Lesson 4: Soloing Over a Jazz Blues

This jazz blues solo example features one of the defining characteristics of jazz: *chromaticism*. In this case, notes that are non-diatonic to the key have been used to connect and approach chord tones and chord tensions by way of half steps. The function of these notes is best described by the term chromatic approach tones. Approach tones can resolve to a targeted note from below, above, or a combination of both. For example, take a look at the B♭ note on the third bar of the tune. This note is approached by one half-step from below and two half-steps from above. Try to see how many chromatic approach tones you can find in this example. The recording on the CD features the rhythm section alone the second time through, so you can practice soloing.

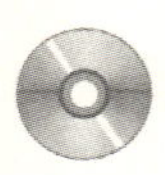

Bebop Blues Solo

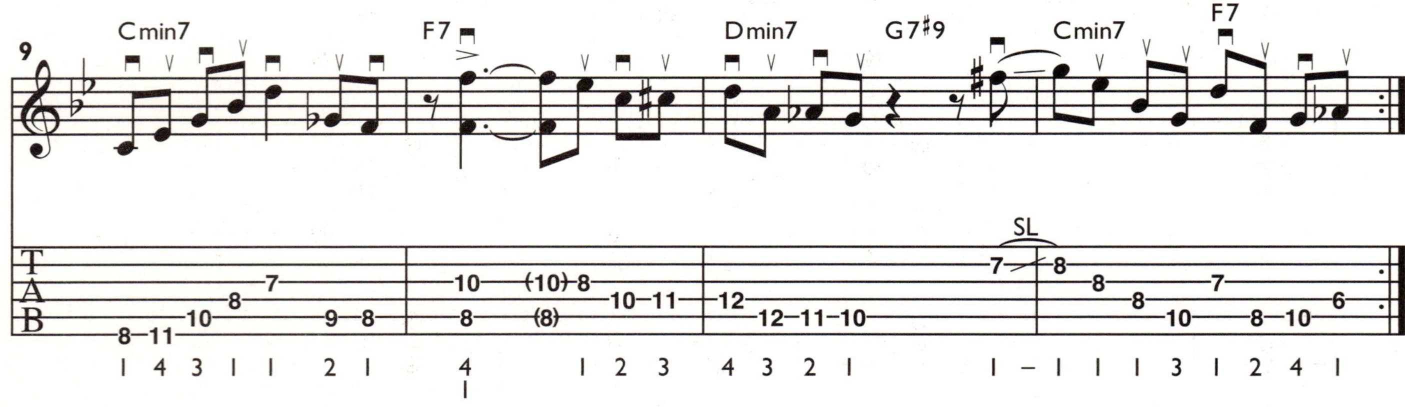

Lesson 5: Jazz Chord Inversions

One of the most effective ways to build up an extensive jazz chord vocabulary is to learn the inversions for chords you already know. Inversions shuffle the notes of a chord to create different bass notes (they usually provide new melody notes too). *First inversion* places the 3rd in the bass, *second inversion* places the 5th in the bass, and *third inversion* places the 7th in the bass.

The voicings in the diagrams below have been organized into two types: chords that have their bass note on the 5th string and chords that have their bass note on the 6th string (the melody note for each inversion is also indicated). Now, multiply the voicings on this page by 12 keys and you have 384 chords.

Chord Inversions with Bass Note on the 5th String

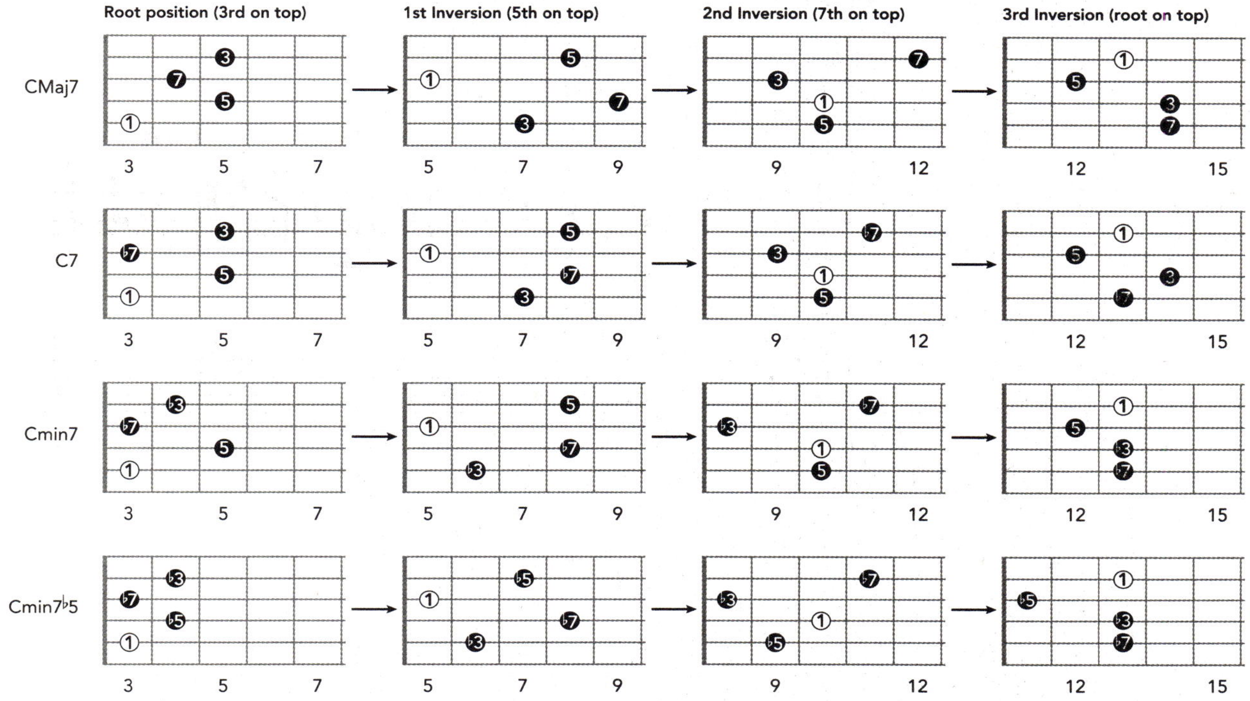

Root position (3rd on top)   1st Inversion (5th on top)   2nd Inversion (7th on top)   3rd Inversion (root on top)

CMaj7

C7

Cmin7

Cmin7♭5

Chord Inversions with Bass Note on the 6th String

Root position (5th on top)   1st Inversion (7th on top)   2nd Inversion (root on top)   3rd Inversion (3rd on top)

GMaj7

G7

Gmin7

Gmin7♭5

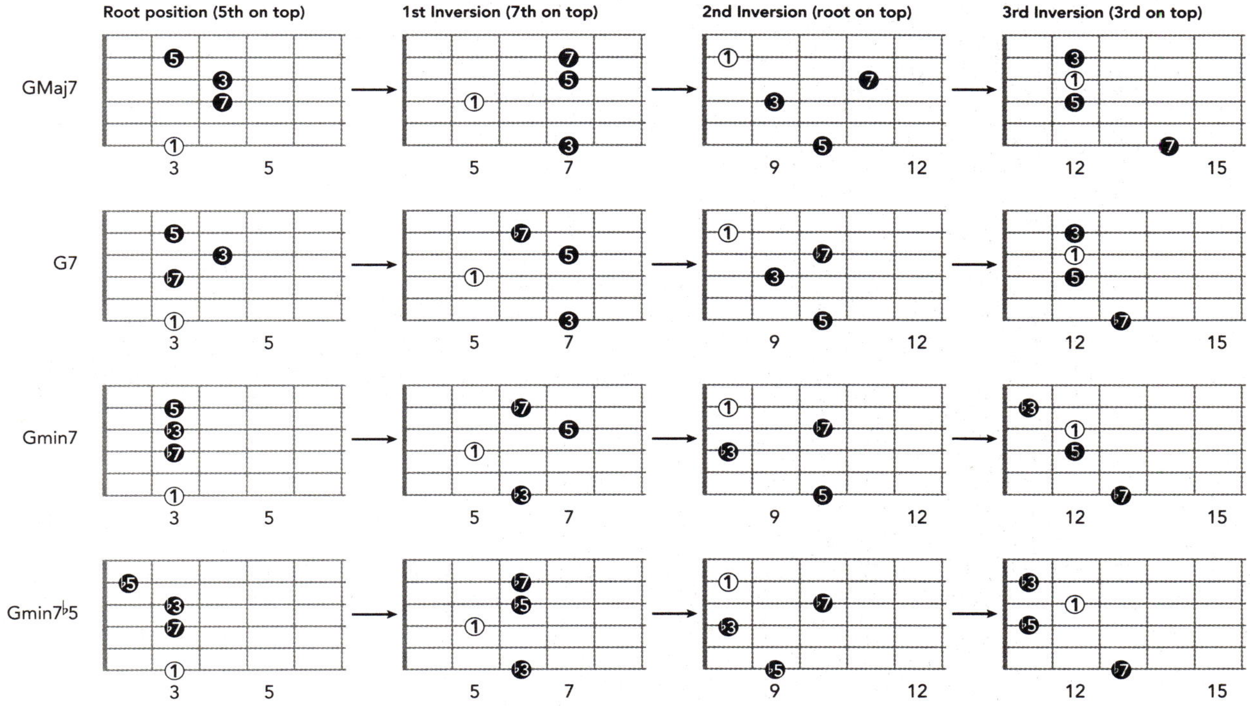

The next example is in the style of the classic jazz standard "Autumn Leaves," composed in 1945. This arrangement is written in the *chord-melody* style of jazz guitar master Joe Pass, and it's played with a *rubato* (rhythmically flexible) time feel. The chord-melody style integrates the harmony and melody into a single guitar part.

The chords in this piece are taken entirely from the inversions introduced on the previous page. When strung together thoughtfully, these chord inversions create smooth bass movement, compelling voice leading, and strong melodies. Plus, when you combine chord inversions with *passing tones* and *chromatic approach* notes, the melodic possibilities are endless.

Fall Inversions

Track 92

     The Guitar Style Resource

Lesson 6: Adding Color to Your Chords

Some jazz compositions call for specific chord voicings and arrangements. However, the vast majority of jazz tunes contain a loose framework of chord changes that are open to spontaneous alteration by the improvising musician. To become a truly versatile jazz guitarist, it's important to work towards building a mental library of colorful chords you can use in place of stock chord changes. The voicings illustrated below are a great place to start.

These chord diagrams are organized by basic chord type, and even though available color tones are dictated by complex considerations like chord function, context, and personal taste, the substitute chords below are applicable to most situations. Also, make sure to pay special attention to the chord formulas and scale degree locations indicated on each voicing so you can construct your own colorful jazz chords on different string sets and fret locations. Altered dominant 7th chords (typically used as $V7$ chords in a minor key) and miscellaneous chord voicings (which you might occasionally come across in a jazz chord chart) are included at the bottom of the page.

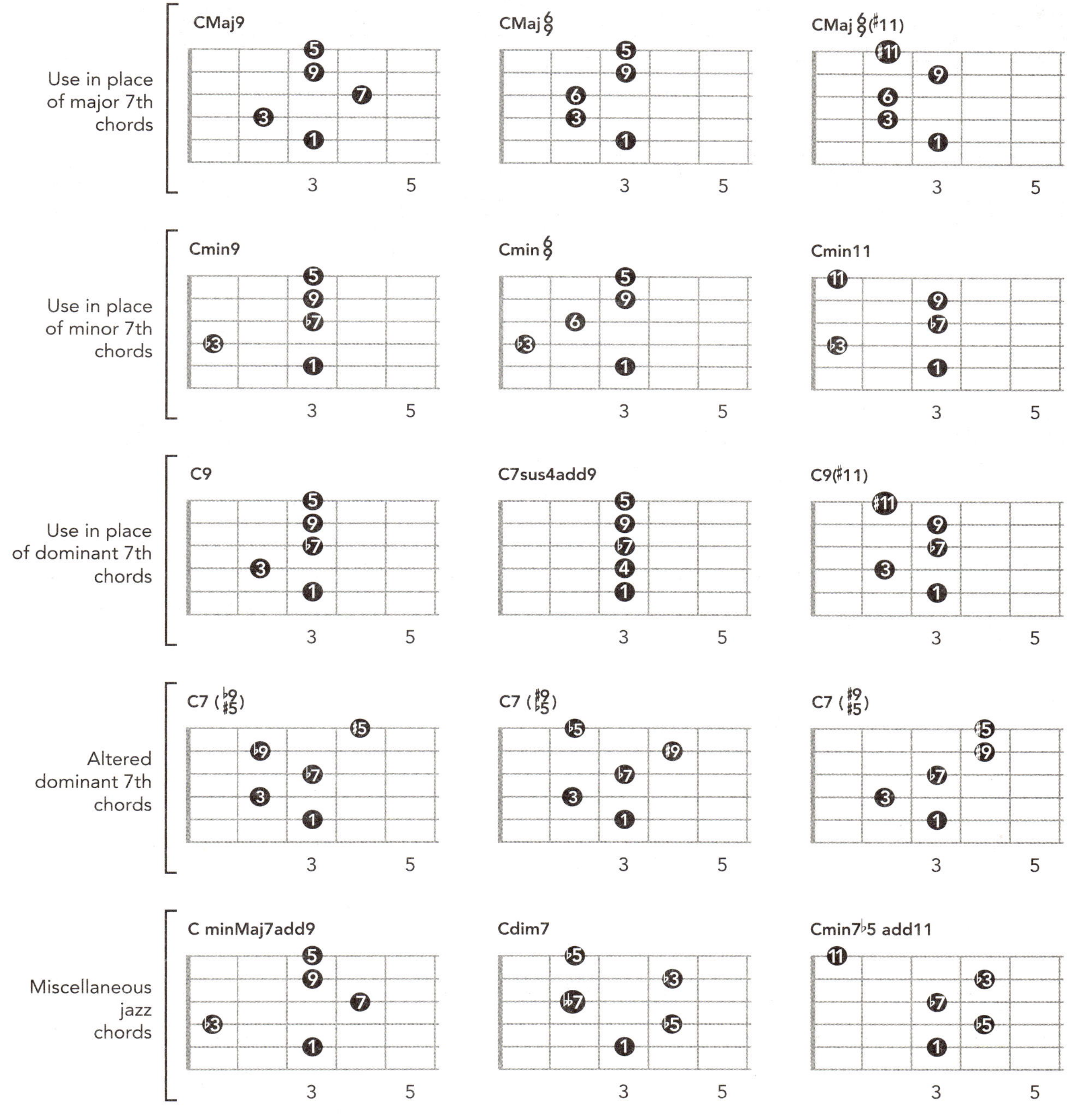

Lesson 7: Latin Jazz

One of the most significant styles of Latin jazz is the bossa nova, made popular in the early 1960s through the celebrated compositions of Brazilian maestro Antônio Carlos Jobim. In particular, nylon string guitar legends João Gilberto and Charlie Byrd played a formative role in defining the bossa nova sound. The following tune, in the style of Jobim's classic "How Insensitive," starts with a basic bossa nova fingerpicking pattern, then proceeds through a few choice rhythmic variations. It features many of the chord voicings introduced on the previous page.

How Syncopated

Track 93

    The Guitar Style Resource

Lesson 8: Modal Jazz

Modal jazz began in the late 1950s as a reaction against the fast-moving chord changes and vertical soloing style of bebop. (*Vertical soloing* is an approach based on arpeggiating each chord in a tune). During this pivotal period, jazz musicians started to loosen what they viewed as harmonic constraints by exploring a more melodic approach to improvisation. Artists like Miles Davis and John Coltrane paved the way for modal jazz by composing pieces written entirely within a single scale or mode. To illustrate this style, check out the following tune written in the style of "So What" by Miles Davis, released in 1959 on what some people call the greatest jazz album of all time, *Kind of Blue*. This example has an AABA form with eight bars of D Dorian, four bars of E♭ Dorian, then another four bars of D Dorian.

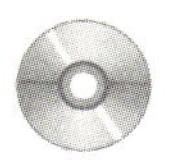

Modal Impression

Track 94

The chord voicings in the modal tune above are unique because they are all comprised of a stack of diatonic 4ths with a diatonic 3rd between the top two notes. These were the voicings used by jazz piano legend Bill Evans on the original "So What" recording. Chords that are built entirely from stacked 4ths are called *quartal voicings*. The good news is, not only do these chords sound amazing, but they also fit very well on the guitar fretboard. To illustrate this, take a look at the diagram below, and you'll see an entire D Dorian scale harmonized in quartal voicings. These chords often sound best when you string them together in a row, so be sure to visualize these shapes in relation to the tonal center for easy key transposition.

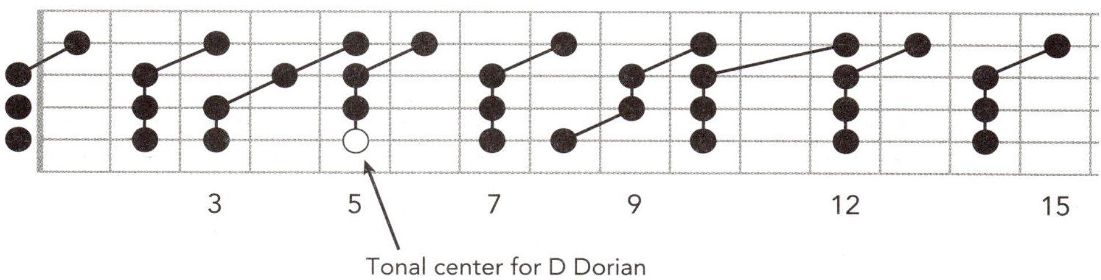

The importance of modes in jazz, and other styles of music as well, cannot be over-emphasized. Understanding the distinguishing characteristics of the modes can provide an insight into how various moods are created in music. The main thing to keep in mind is that modes can be rationalized in two ways: in a *parallel* sense and a *relative* sense.

To build modes in a parallel way, start with the major scale (the Ionian mode) and modify it with appropriate scale degree alterations. For example, take a G Major scale and lower the 7th scale degree, and you've constructed the G Mixolydian mode. To build modes in a relative way, designate the appropriate scale degree of the major scale as the desired tonal center. For example, visualize the 5th scale degree of the G Major scale (the note D) as your tonal center, and you've built the D Mixolydian mode. With both methods, you will end up with the same collection of notes. The diagram below illustrates all seven modes of the G Major scale.

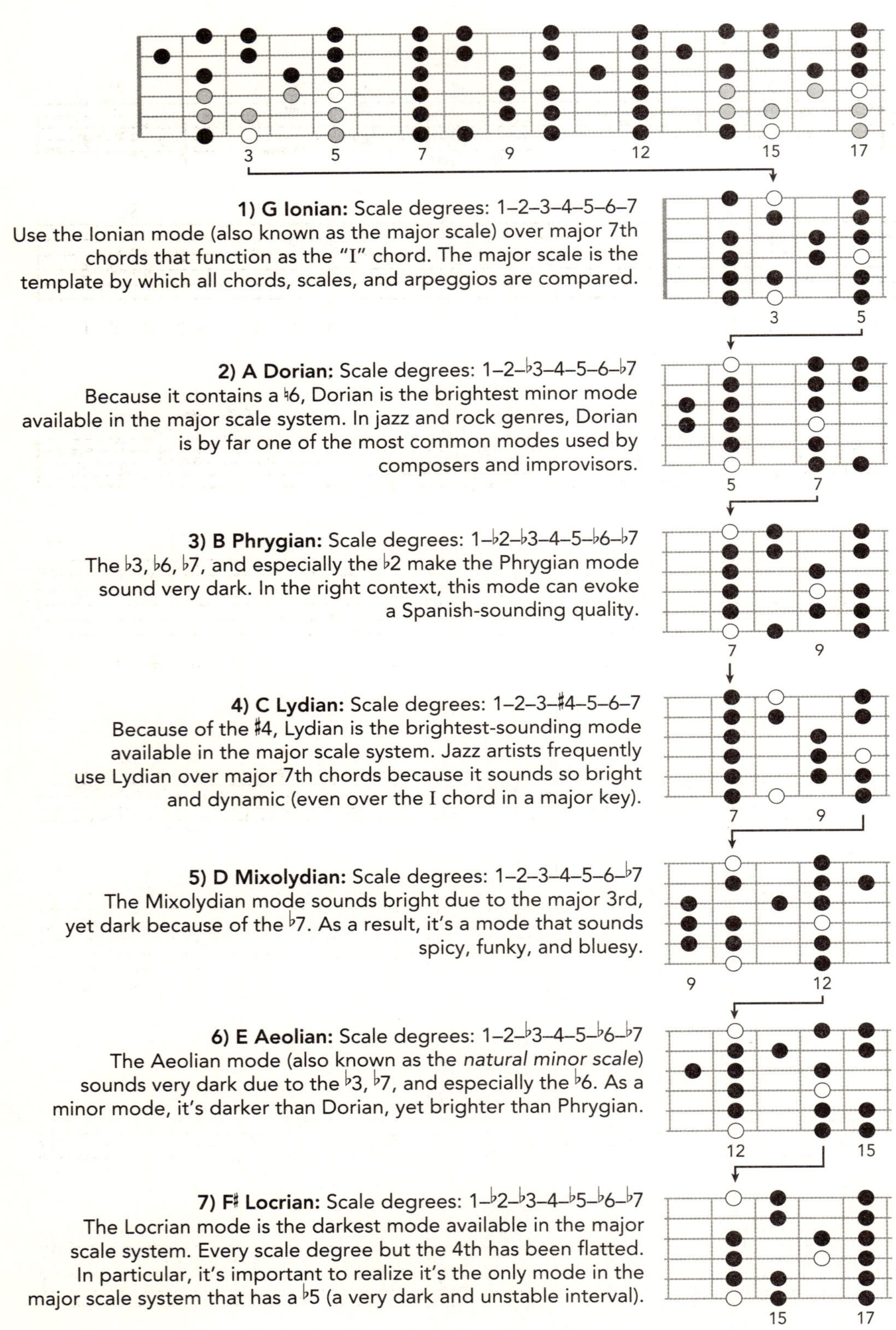

1) G Ionian: Scale degrees: 1–2–3–4–5–6–7
Use the Ionian mode (also known as the major scale) over major 7th chords that function as the "I" chord. The major scale is the template by which all chords, scales, and arpeggios are compared.

2) A Dorian: Scale degrees: 1–2–♭3–4–5–6–♭7
Because it contains a ♮6, Dorian is the brightest minor mode available in the major scale system. In jazz and rock genres, Dorian is by far one of the most common modes used by composers and improvisors.

3) B Phrygian: Scale degrees: 1–♭2–♭3–4–5–♭6–♭7
The ♭3, ♭6, ♭7, and especially the ♭2 make the Phrygian mode sound very dark. In the right context, this mode can evoke a Spanish-sounding quality.

4) C Lydian: Scale degrees: 1–2–3–♯4–5–6–7
Because of the ♯4, Lydian is the brightest-sounding mode available in the major scale system. Jazz artists frequently use Lydian over major 7th chords because it sounds so bright and dynamic (even over the I chord in a major key).

5) D Mixolydian: Scale degrees: 1–2–3–4–5–6–♭7
The Mixolydian mode sounds bright due to the major 3rd, yet dark because of the ♭7. As a result, it's a mode that sounds spicy, funky, and bluesy.

6) E Aeolian: Scale degrees: 1–2–♭3–4–5–♭6–♭7
The Aeolian mode (also known as the *natural minor scale*) sounds very dark due to the ♭3, ♭7, and especially the ♭6. As a minor mode, it's darker than Dorian, yet brighter than Phrygian.

7) F♯ Locrian: Scale degrees: 1–♭2–♭3–4–♭5–♭6–♭7
The Locrian mode is the darkest mode available in the major scale system. Every scale degree but the 4th has been flatted. In particular, it's important to realize it's the only mode in the major scale system that has a ♭5 (a very dark and unstable interval).

Lesson 9: Modal Jazz Soloing

In modal soloing, one of the most effective devices used by jazz masters is targeting color tones. These are the tones that give the mode its distinguishing characteristics (as covered on the previous page). Since this a Dorian example, targeting the 2, 4, and 6 (otherwise known as the 9, 11, and 13) is just as important as targeting the chord tones. This example also utilizes harmonic anticipation. This device is featured in bar 8 and the last half of bar 12, where notes of the approaching key are played before the key change is actually made, creating a very modern sound. The music on the CD repeats with just the rhythm section, so you can practice soloing over the changes.

Tonal Modal

Track 95

Lesson 10: Jazz Soloing Strategies

We've covered a lot of territory so far. It's time to kick back and have some fun. The examples that follow are all song snippets based on the chord changes of famous jazz standards. Scale diagrams are included to facilitate smooth key and mode changes. Try to make melodies and phrases with these scale shapes and you will be improvising while making the changes. Good luck, and most importantly—have fun and enjoy these sophisticated jazz sounds.

The following example is an uptempo modal jazz progression that features two modes: D Mixolydian and D Lydian. The scale fingerings are placed in roughly the same area, illustrating how to play over two different modes without changing fretboard position.

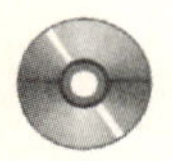

Maybe

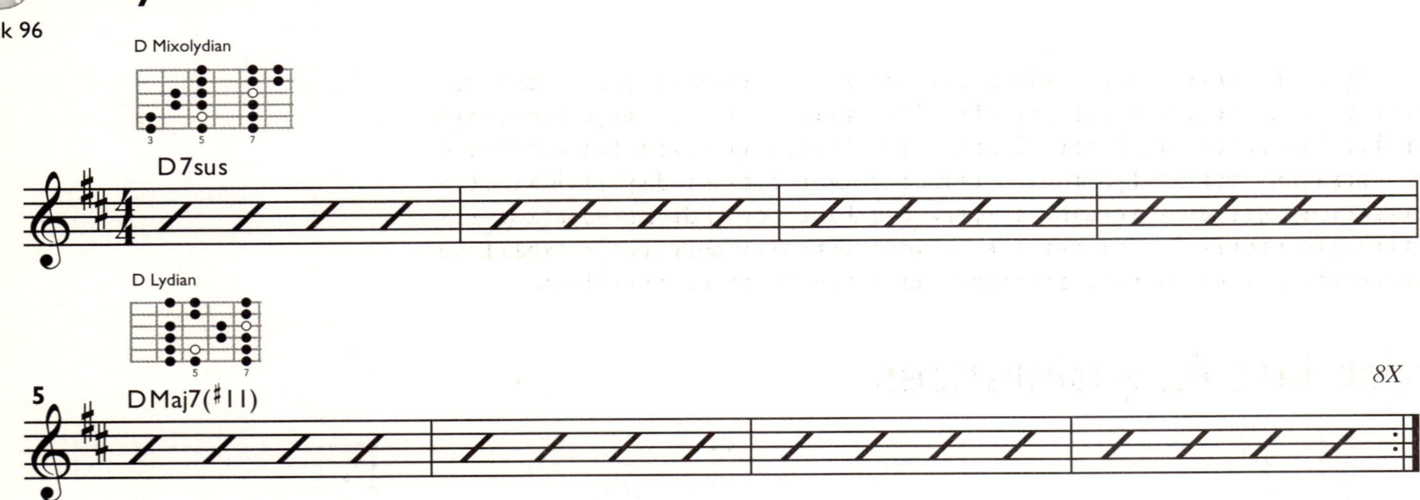

The scale diagrams in the example below illustrate how to solo over four different tonalities of the Lydian mode with a single scale shape. As the tonal centers descend in whole steps, a single Lydian scale shape descends along with it.

Outward Inclination

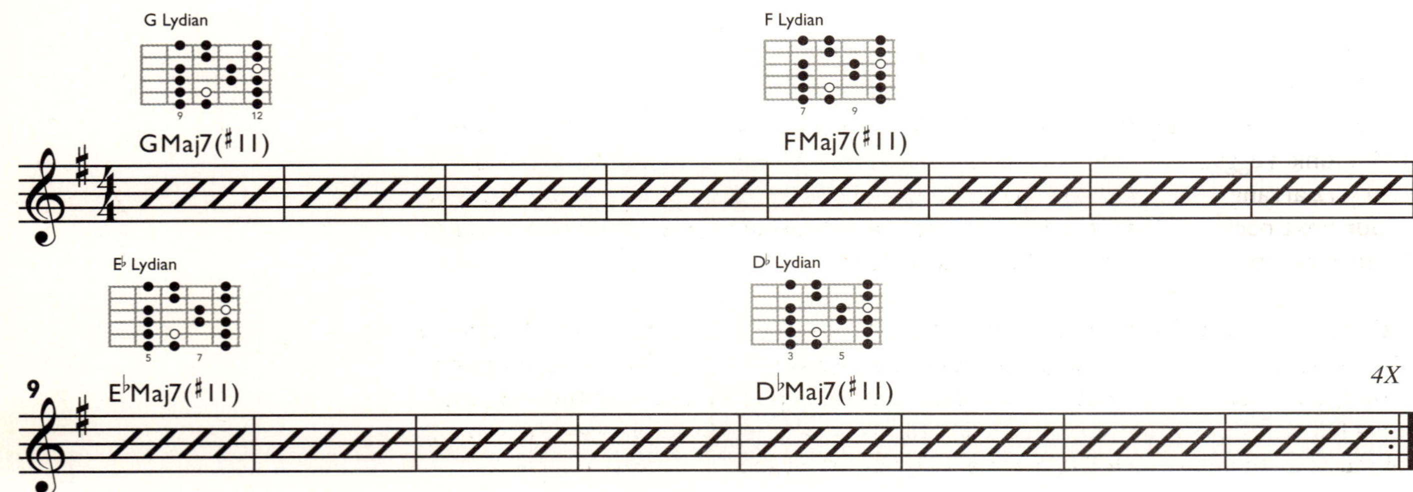

The following example is a modal jazz ballad. In this case, the switch from D♭ Ionian to A Lydian is a fairly drastic change because there are relatively few common tones between the two modes. However, the transition is simplified by staying in the same fretboard position.

Yellow Noon

Track 98

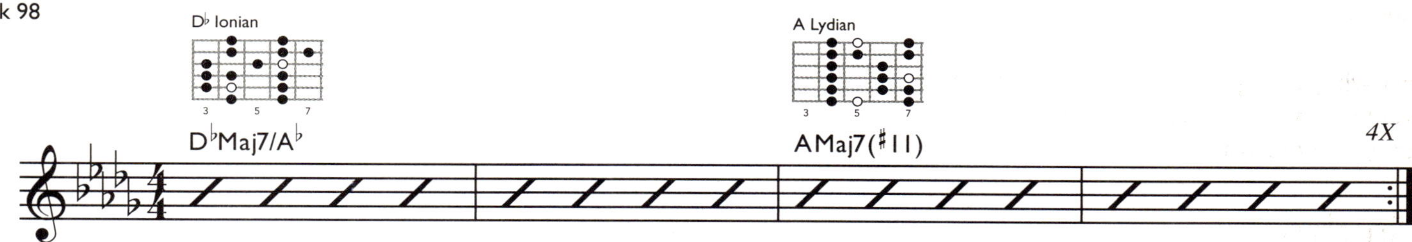

This final eight-bar example is played with a Latin jazz feel at a moderate tempo. Upon close inspection of this chord progression, you'll find that it's not as tricky to navigate as it might seem at first. This is due to the fact that C Dorian and F Mixolydian are actually the same scale pattern. Take a close look at C Lydian and G Ionian, and you'll notice that they are also identical. On a separate note, as you explore this tune, pay special attention to the *altered scale* (the last mode in the progression). Try out this scale and your ears will instantly start to expand; it is, without a doubt, one of the most sophisticated sounds available to jazz improvisers.

Not Just Acquaintances

Track 99

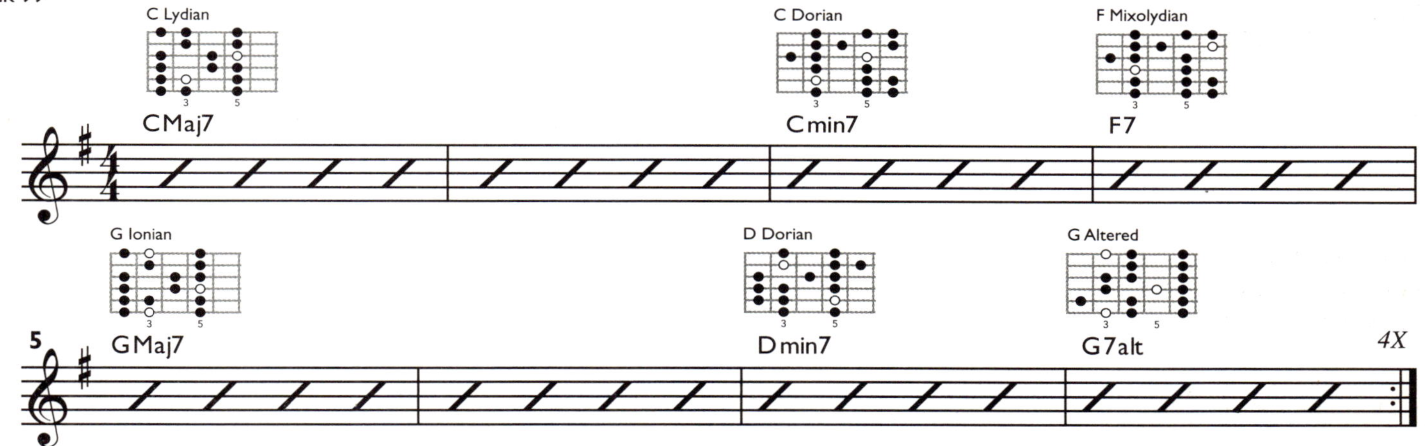

Conclusion

Congratulations! By studying the pages of this book, you now have a solid grasp of rhythmic genres like funk, reggae, and ska. In addition, you know what chords and scales to use in your next jazz arrangement, and you have a deep grab bag of licks and techniques ready to use at your next rock or blues jam. In short, you now have the tools to excel as a skilled soloist and accompanist in a variety of musical styles.

But that's not all. From the heavy crunch of a speed metal gallop to the relaxing groove of the bossa nova, you now have a glimpse of the enormous freedom and wisdom gained by choosing the wide road of musical versatility. But, it's up to you to take the next step. To get the full benefit of your newfound skills, be sure to listen to and appreciate as many types of music as possible: melodic, harmonic, lyrical, rhythmic, and experimental.

Without a doubt, the most direct path to musical versatility is an open mind. Good luck and have fun!

GUITAR FRETBOARD CHART
Frets 1–12

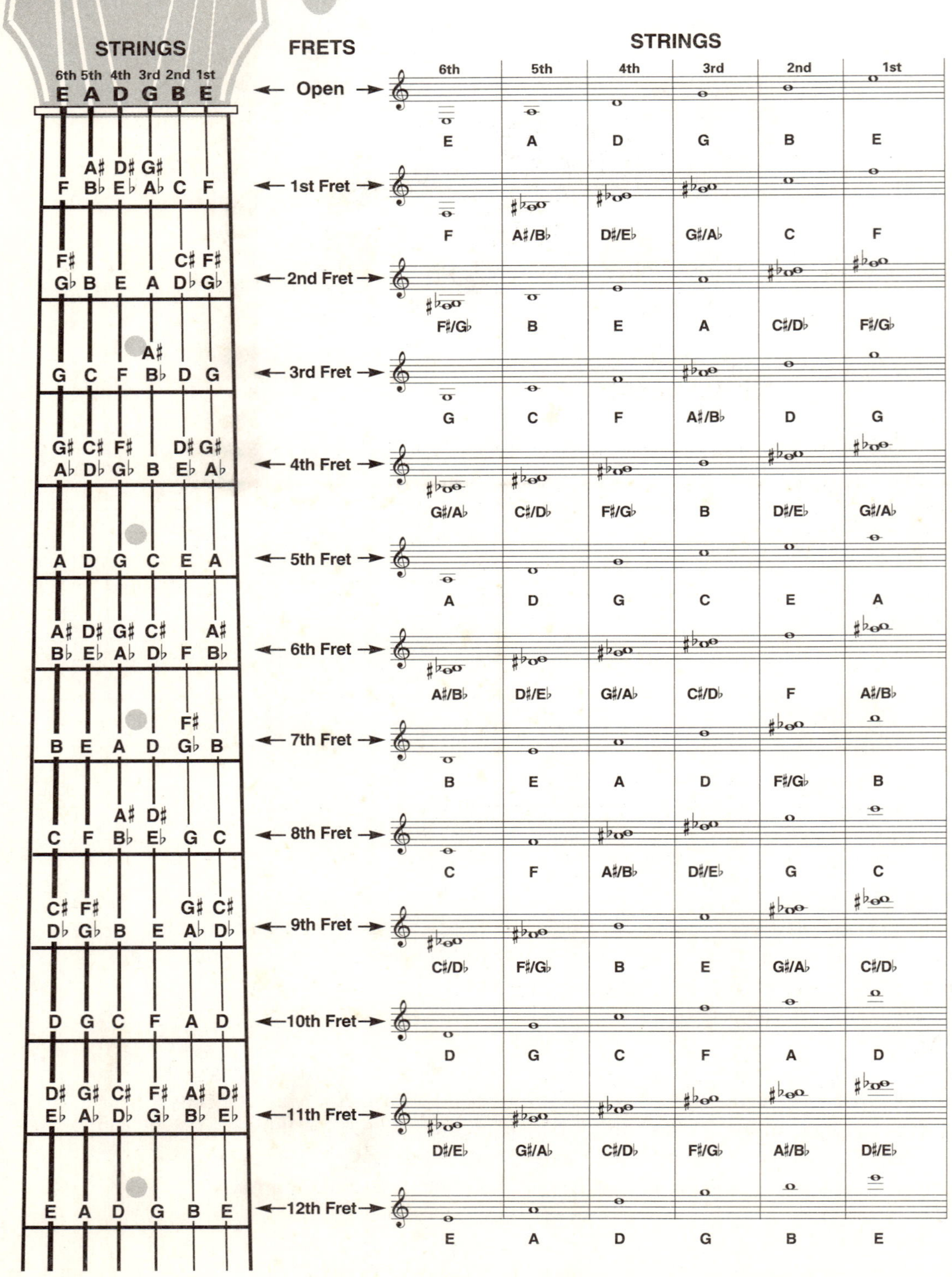

STRINGS

Fret	6th	5th	4th	3rd	2nd	1st
Open	E	A	D	G	B	E
1st Fret	F	A#/Bb	D#/Eb	G#/Ab	C	F
2nd Fret	F#/Gb	B	E	A	C#/Db	F#/Gb
3rd Fret	G	C	F	A#/Bb	D	G
4th Fret	G#/Ab	C#/Db	F#/Gb	B	D#/Eb	G#/Ab
5th Fret	A	D	G	C	E	A
6th Fret	A#/Bb	D#/Eb	G#/Ab	C#/Db	F	A#/Bb
7th Fret	B	E	A	D	F#/Gb	B
8th Fret	C	F	A#/Bb	D#/Eb	G	C
9th Fret	C#/Db	F#/Gb	B	E	G#/Ab	C#/Db
10th Fret	D	G	C	F	A	D
11th Fret	D#/Eb	G#/Ab	C#/Db	F#/Gb	A#/Bb	D#/Eb
12th Fret	E	A	D	G	B	E